# STARTING
# OUT
# RIGHT

# STARTING
# OUT
# RIGHT

*A Proven Financial Strategy
for Young Couples*

# LARRY
# BURKETT

David C Cook®
*transforming lives together*

STARTING OUT RIGHT
Published by David C Cook
4050 Lee Vance View
Colorado Springs, CO 80918 U.S.A.

David C Cook Distribution Canada
55 Woodslee Avenue, Paris, Ontario, Canada N3L 3E5

David C Cook U.K., Kingsway Communications
Eastbourne, East Sussex BN23 6NT, England

The graphic circle C logo is a registered trademark of David C Cook.

The website addresses recommended throughout this book are offered as a
resource to you. These websites are not intended in any way to be or imply an
endorsement on the part of David C Cook, nor do we vouch for their content.

All Scripture quotations are taken from the New American
Standard Bible®, Copyright © 1960, 1995
by The Lockman Foundation. Used by permission. (www.Lockman.org.)
The author has added italics to Scripture quotations for emphasis.

LCCN 2015945899
ISBN 978-0-7814-1266-7
eISBN 978-0-7814-1377-0

© 1989, 2015 Lawrence Burkett Sr.
First edition published as *The Complete Financial Guide for Young Couples*
in 1989 © Larry Burkett/Allen Burkett, ISBN 978-1-56476-130-9

The Team: Alex Field, Tim Peterson, Ingrid Beck, Tiffany
Thomas, Amy Konyndyk, Karen Athen
Cover Design: Nick Lee
Cover Photo: Shutterstock

Printed in the United States of America
Second Edition 2015

1 2 3 4 5 6 7 8 9 10

080415

# CONTENTS

# FOREWORD

"Do not worry," Jesus said several times in Matthew 6:19–34. The context shows He was talking about money.

Our Lord was not advocating a careless attitude toward our finances. Rather, He was calling us to a level of faith and behavior that is free from money worries.

Married couples in particular would do well to heed His counsel. Statistics show that money trouble is the number one cause of stress and failure in marriages. Christians are not exempt, and one reason appears to be that many Christian couples are oblivious to what the Bible teaches about managing family finances.

Larry Burkett offers an invaluable remedy for this dilemma. *Starting Out Right* is filled with wise and biblical instruction for those who want to know what God's Word says about managing money. Burkett's commonsense approach is neither pedagogical nor theoretical, but lively and practical. In simple, straightforward terms, he unfolds an array of scriptural precepts that will help any Christian couple manage their money more effectively and without anxiety.

Years of experience in teaching and counseling Christian families about finances has uniquely prepared Larry Burkett to write this book. He has witnessed the pitfalls. He has seen countless couples struggle with the same issues. He knows the hazards, and he understands the biblical answers. Best of all, he does a masterful job of making them understandable for others.

And these are principles we had better understand. All of us who are believers face judgment one day regarding what kind of stewards we have been. What too many Christians don't realize is that stewardship involves far more than the money we put in the collection plate. It encompasses every element of how we manage the resources God has blessed us with. Perhaps the most telling testing ground of stewardship is the realm of home finances.

It is significant that one of the basic requirements for a man to be in a position of spiritual leadership is that "he must be one who manages his own household well" (1 Tim. 3:4). Our Lord even taught that the quality of our stewardship in this life will determine our reward in the next (see Matt. 25:14–30). The simple fact is that we cannot be truly effective for God if we fail to manage our finances well.

The Enemy knows this, and perhaps that is why he seems to work so hard to snare young families and render them ineffective through unwise spending, lack of discipline, debt, worry, and other problems related to money.

If you're experiencing any of those difficulties, whether you're just starting out or approaching the crisis point, this book is for you. It will revolutionize the way you view your finances. If you practice the principles it teaches, you'll discover how to glorify God through managing your money wisely, and you'll take an important step toward living without anxiety.

*John F. MacArthur Jr.*
*Grace Community Church*
*Sun Valley, California*

# NOTE FROM THE PUBLISHER

Dear Reader,

Larry Burkett was a respected financial counselor and adviser who was truly loved by all those whose lives he touched: his family, his friends, and his ministry partners. He lived a life of Christian kindness and genuine humility. He was always extraordinarily generous. One of the central principles Larry taught is that we don't really own things; we are simply stewards and managers of what God has entrusted to us. In Larry's case, that included the ministry he founded, which became Crown Financial Ministries.

Larry was also a prolific writer, authoring more than seventy books including several bestsellers as well as the book you hold in your hands, which was originally titled *The Complete Financial Guide for Young Couples*. Because we feel the principles in this book still have relevance and practical application in today's world, we are re-releasing this book under a new title, *Starting Out Right: A Proven Financial Strategy for Young Couples*.

Though we have done our best to update any outdated content, there may still be a few areas where Larry uses financial examples that don't reflect the financial realities you are facing. However, we feel strongly that the financial principles Larry outlines in this book will provide you with a wise and circumspect approach to establishing your finances. If you have additional questions on the principles outlined in this book, we invite you to go to the Crown Financial Ministries website: www.crown.org.

*May you be blessed as you seek to honor*
*God with your finances,*


*The Editorial Staff at David C Cook*

# PART ONE

# DEVELOPING A SHORT-RANGE PLAN

# INTRODUCTION

Finances are an important part of marriage. Unfortunately, mismanagement of money accounts for the majority of divorces in America today. That should make this problem a critical issue for most husbands and wives. But for some reason, that's not the case.

The average marriage that ends in divorce starts out just about like anybody else's. These couples have high expectations; they really love each other. Sadly, their inability to make good financial decisions leads them down the road to disaster.

Wouldn't it be great if, in America today, divorce was limited only to non-Christians? But unfortunately, it is not. That says something: most Christian couples are just as ignorant about finances as non-Christian couples. Divorce, bankruptcy, and debt within the Christian community indicate that our priorities are mixed up and that we are omitting some vital training for our children.

The average young husband and wife try to accumulate in about three years what should take them thirty years to accumulate. Consequently, what they do accumulate is an enormous amount of debt. As a result of the debt, they have financial pressures; and as a result of the financial pressures, they stop communicating. They cease to be companions and, instead, they become combatants. When they talk, it's about financial problems. They don't bother to read their

Bibles anymore; it's hard to study the Bible when your mind is consumed with problems. They don't pray anymore; it's hard to pray when your mind is consumed with problems. Allow me to illustrate.

A young couple I'll call Bob and Sue met in college and married when Bob graduated. Sue came from a Christian home, and Bob was saved through a campus ministry when he was a college freshman. After college, Bob went to work in a stock brokerage firm and began to do quite well. His first year he made nearly $30,000 in commissions. Consequently, Bob and Sue felt they could commit to buying a home, which they did. Sue's parents loaned them the down payment. With closing costs, attorney fees, and so on, they owed another $1,500, which they put on their credit card.

Next came the usual household expenses for drapes, furniture, lawn mower, and appliances. Even so, they might have been able to squeeze by if everything had gone just right—which it didn't.

Their five-year-old car broke down, as it did regularly, so Bob bought a new car by selling his old car, borrowing some money from his parents, and taking out a $6,000 car loan at 18 percent interest. Although neither Bob nor Sue realized it at the time, they had stepped into one of Satan's modern traps, just as surely as Eve had in the garden. Satan asked Eve, "Indeed, has God said, 'You shall not eat from any tree of the garden'?" (Gen. 3:1). Today he asks, "Surely you can trust God for the good things you need, can't you?" And using about the same wisdom as Adam and Eve, Bob and Sue borrowed to buy things they couldn't afford to own. Satan then had them hooked, and all he needed to do was wait until the line played out.

Bob and Sue's line played out when Sue unexpectedly got pregnant about six months after moving into their new home. Frequent bouts of morning sickness caused her to take a leave of absence from her job. Then the downhill financial slide started. Without Sue's income, the house and car payments alone took 70 percent of their pay. After food, gas, utilities, and the other monthly essentials, no money was left for clothes, entertainment, lunches, and, least of all, medical expenses.

Every trip to the doctor meant prescription bills and non-reimbursed expenses, and every trip resulted in an argument over money or, more accurately, the lack of it. What should have been a joyful event was soon to be a disaster.

About three months into the pregnancy, the economy soured for stock investing and Bob lost his job. He was out of work for nearly two months, during which time virtually all bills went unpaid. Bob eventually found another job, making about $18,000 a year, with a budget that required more than $40,000 just to break even.

When the baby was born, Bob and Sue were separated and she was living with her parents. The young couple lost their home and their new car and still owed nearly $16,000—all in less than three years of marriage.

Maybe you're thinking, *Well, that won't happen to me*, or *It's already too late for us*. Neither is true. God's Word has both the prevention and the cure. If you haven't made the errors yet, you have a head start. But even if you have, God's Word offers the absolute cure.

Jesus dedicated about two-thirds of all parables in the New Testament to teaching the principles of how to handle money properly. Have you ever had somebody take the time to teach you how to handle money properly? If you have, you're among the fortunate few.

What I would like to do is spend some time discussing practical principles of finances. First we'll look at the biblical basis for why we are to handle money properly. Then we'll look at the practical applications in everyday life, like balancing checkbooks, buying life insurance, selecting the right house, or buying the car you "need." Hopefully, by the time you finish this book, you'll have the necessary tools to handle your finances properly.

How important is money? About 80 percent of our waking day is consumed in thinking about money: making it, saving it, spending it, or giving it away. If this area isn't managed properly, everything else is out of balance. "He who is faithful in a very little thing is faithful also in much; and he who is unrighteous in a very little thing is unrighteous also in much" (Luke 16:10).

# 1   GOD'S WISDOM

In order to discuss financial management properly, I need to back up and start with the source of all wisdom, God's Word. I'd like to bring into focus the difference between how God says we should handle money and what the world has been teaching us about handling money.

I have been a Christian for about nineteen years, prior to which I was a non-Christian for about thirty years, including the first eleven years of my marriage. My wife, Judy, and I were a typical young couple. She came from a fairly well-to-do family, and I came from a fairly "poor-to-do" family. I thought she would be a spendthrift; therefore, I sought to control all the finances in our marriage. As you might imagine, we argued—a lot. You might say we had communication problems, most of them related to finances, and yet we never really lacked money. Ours was a lack of understanding about how God uses opposites in a marriage. But I'll come back to that later.

When we were first married, I would remind my wife (regularly) not to leave lights on, to turn the heat down, and not to leave the refrigerator door open. It wasn't really a conscious thing. It was my defense against what I presumed to be her latent desire to cost me money. One time, without her knowing about it, I unscrewed the lightbulb in the refrigerator so she would think the light had burned out. Now, that's pretty cheap.

In fact, when we were first married, I would tell Judy, "I'm a basically frugal person," especially when she mentioned buying clothes. Then, a couple of years later, she said, "You're a basically cheap person, and there's a difference." Ever since that time, I have tried to be frugal, not cheap.

I now realize that God has put Judy in my life to help provide the balance I need, and vice versa. Without her I would never buy furniture, and without me she would never change the oil in the car, both of which are necessary.

We were both unsaved when we got married. Consequently, we had only experience to fall back on in working out our relationship together, and most of that was bad. Our greatest asset prior to becoming Christians was that we had no other place to go, so we stuck it out together. Only when we came to know Christ did we begin to realize that God's Word has basic principles governing every aspect of a marriage, including finances.

One of the first things I realized as I began to read God's Word was the contrast between what the Bible taught about money and what I had been taught in business school. The primary principle taught throughout most business schools is called OPM. It means Other People's Money. In our economy today it might also be described as the credit mentality—the ability to borrow that allows people to buy things they cannot afford to own. That principle works great in good times. Early in a marriage, it will allow you to accumulate a lot of things you otherwise couldn't afford. Unfortunately, later you'll have a real problem with that philosophy.

The classic example of that in our society today can be seen in the plight of America's farmers. Many young farmers came out of agricultural schools that taught OPM. They inherited farms that were debt-free and profitable. But with ever-appreciating land values, they were convinced that it was old-fashioned and foolish to sit on a farm with all that equity in it.

So initially they borrowed to upgrade the operation: better planters, better tractors, barns, silos. Every farming magazine carried glowing articles on the progressive farmers who turned idle equity into operating capital. Then the borrowing expanded to buy more land, which increased in value and could, in turn, be leveraged. Borrowed capital funded new homes, air-conditioned harvesters, new trucks, vacations. Farmers were on a roll. Eventually, the debts got so large that farmers borrowed to make interest payments, and so little cash was left over at the end of a season that they had to borrow to buy seed for the next. At this point they knew they were in trouble, but they were trapped by the very debt they had used to build too quickly.

Ultimately, the crisis came. Farm produce prices dropped and, with them, land prices collapsed. The debt on many farms exceeded their total value, sometimes by a factor of three or four to one. Panicked by the turn of events, bankers cut off all credit and farmers couldn't even plant for the next season.

Thousands of families were evicted, and farms that had been in the same families for generations were auctioned off for a fraction of their accumulated debt. Any one of those families would have been thrilled to go back to where they began, but it was too late. Their problem was not stupidity. Most are very intelligent people with good academic educations. Their problem was ignorance: a lack of understanding. They had been taught well, but they had been taught the wrong things.

This same fundamental error is being repeated in millions of young families today. They build too much too quickly, using too much debt, and when they hit a down stretch—and everybody does eventually—they get wiped out just like the farmers.

Let me make it very clear: we have been taught false principles by the world in which we live. The plumb line for truth is God's Word, not a college textbook or a standard practice.

God's Word teaches a set of principles most of us haven't heard in the media or in the classroom. For example, what is the first thing that comes to your mind when I say, "There goes a very wealthy person"? You visualize someone with a surplus of money, large cars, maybe a large business, and certainly a large home. That's the normal image of wealth in our society. But when God's Word describes a wealthy person, it never makes reference to the accumulation of money. God's Word says that wealth is more than money. Wealth is everything that you and I have as Christians.

Our greatest wealth from God is salvation. It never ends. The friends we have are part of our wealth from God. Our children are a part of our inheritance. Even the relationship between a husband and wife (in the Lord) is a part of our wealth from God.

So as you evaluate the difference between God's wealth and the world's wealth, you begin to realize that God promises riches, honor, and a long life. But the riches God refers to are not just money. He desires that you have peace along with your riches.

If you don't settle early in your marriage that money is never going to make you happy, you'll spend your entire life doing urgent things, rather than important things, and find at age seventy that you spent your whole life chasing after the Joneses only to discover that, when you finally caught up with them, they had refinanced.

I have counseled many people throughout the years. Some were senior citizens who went from marriage to marriage themselves and then saw their children go from marriage to marriage. Most of them looked back on their lives with great regret. Often they said, "If only I had heard that fifty years ago. If only somebody had sat me down and told me what to do, what a difference it would have made in my life." Well, maybe it would have and maybe it wouldn't have, but at least you have the opportunity to hear truth now!

The principles and practices that we're going to discuss are not just suggestions from God's Word. They are truths that you must apply to your life. They help focus your life on doing important things, not just urgent things. The urgent things include your job, a new car, a bigger home, a better vacation. The important things are how you're investing your lives together, husband and wife, and what kind of a spiritual legacy you'll leave your children's children. "A good man leaves an inheritance to his children's children" (Prov. 13:22).

It's interesting that Jesus lived among a generation of people who had very little money. In fact, Matthew was probably one of the few disciples who had any money at all, because he had been a tax collector. Yet, in teaching those men, Jesus consistently developed His parables (a teaching technique where a well-known topic is used to relate to a little-understood topic) around the handling of money. Jesus chose money because it is a common denominator among all people, regardless of age, sex, or race.

It's hard to think of another area of life that touches virtually everyone they are married or single, young or old. It's amazing that for such a long time Christians have failed to see the relationship between handling finances and other areas of struggle.

# 2    MONEY: AN OUTSIDE INDICATOR

In the New Testament, Jesus draws an interesting parallel between the way we handle our money and the way we handle spiritual matters. In fact, the way we handle our money is the best outside reflection of our true inner values. You can tell more about the spiritual lives of a couple by looking at their checkbook than by anything else. People can say anything they think others want to hear, and many people are great at faking their true attitudes, but the way they handle their finances is usually a dead giveaway to what is *really* going on.

One of the things I learned in counseling a long time ago is this: always counsel a married couple together because you'll get much better answers from two than you will from just one. Most people are usually somewhat self-conscious about their financial mistakes. As a result, they tend to water down their abuses, particularly where debts are concerned. Also, since most couples are opposites, one tends to exaggerate, while the other has a very narrow sense of the truth. Between the two of them, the right balance can be found.

A few years ago, while at my desk working on an upcoming conference, I received a call from an obviously distressed young woman named Becky.

"They're coming to repossess our home," she said. "Can you help us, please?"

It took me several minutes to get her calmed down enough to explain what was happening. It seemed her husband paid the bills (or was supposed to), but he was consistently negligent about details—such as mailing the checks! Almost every month he was late with the mortgage payment and, consequently, had accumulated several months of late charges, which he refused to pay. The mortgage company had decided to take a hard stand and started foreclosure proceedings.

We scheduled an impromptu counseling session later that day. Steve and Becky were the classic opposites. She was a perfectionist who followed rules to the letter. He was so creative and footloose that he sometimes forgot where he put his paycheck. Because of her personality, Becky tended to see everything in black and white. To her, a foreclosure notice meant she was going to be evicted. Steve, on the other hand, simply occupied his thoughts elsewhere. His plan was to mail in the late charges at the last possible moment. It seemed perfectly justifiable to him. He was making the mortgage company "sweat," he said. In truth, he was violating his promise to pay on time and was creating unnecessary stress for his wife.

As I got to know them better in later counseling sessions, I learned that Steve also cheated on his expense account and rarely, if ever, declared all of his income to the IRS. Steve had a spiritual flaw that was reflected in his finances.

Christ said that if a person is not faithful in the smallest of things (money), he or she will not be faithful in greater things: "He who is faithful in a very little thing is faithful also in much; and he who is unrighteous in a very little thing is unrighteous also in much.

Therefore if you have not been faithful in the use of unrighteous wealth, who will entrust the true riches to you?" (Luke 16:10–11). Jesus repeated that principle several times (see verses 12–13) just to be certain that we couldn't misunderstand or misinterpret it. The way we handle our money is nothing more than the outward expression of what's going on spiritually inside.

Money can be either the best area of communication in your marriage or the worst. It's rarely neutral. If you learn to communicate properly, it can be an excellent means for understanding the assets and liabilities of one another. Remember that being *different* does not mean being inferior. Each personality brings strengths and weaknesses to a marriage. I have seldom met a couple where the husband and wife are carbon copies. If you're too similar, one of you is probably unnecessary. Therefore, opposites usually do attract.

# 3   COMBATANTS OR COMPANIONS?

With rare exception, most couples are so opposite they're predictable. One likes to go to bed late, and one likes to go to bed early. One likes littering, and the other goes around cleaning up. One has a terrible sense of direction, and the other always knows where they are. One wants to invest, and the other wants to spend. I could go on and on because most couples I've met fit the pattern. Opposites *do* attract. But when you use your differences as assets, you'll find that as you communicate about anything, particularly money, you'll get opposite and wise perspectives for making decisions. The goal is to achieve a proper balance in your marriage.

Many times a couple will approach their marriage as combatants because of the differences in their personalities. You were attracted to each other because you were different. One of you never talked at a party, and the other never stopped. So the quiet person who really would like to be more outgoing is attracted to the other because he or she *is* outgoing. But later, if you're not careful, the very things that attracted you will make you resent your partner. It's really a choice—combatants or companions? You're not going to change the other person's personality, nor should you try.

Through counseling many couples over the years, I had determined that there are four basic personality types with many minor variations. I was in the process of sorting through these and categorizing them when I discovered that someone else had already done this, so I just adopted the Personal Profile System of evaluation.

The four basic traits are Dominant, Influencing, Steady, and Conscientious. Each of us possesses some part of all the personality traits, but generally one trait is predominant. Let me give a thumbnail description of each; look for yourself and your spouse as you read.

*Dominant*, or high "D," is a decision maker who likes challenges. This person desires power, authority, and a great deal of individuality. Of this personality it has been said, "Often wrong, but never in doubt." You can recognize this personality because he seldom follows instructions. He is the one who will order a swing set in a box and try to assemble it without reading the instructions.

*Influencing* is the outgoing verbalizer who usually becomes the life of the party. This personality likes recognition and group activity.

You can recognize her by the fact that everything she has ever done can be found on her walls. Where the "D" clams up under pressure, the "I" wants to talk everything out, in great detail.

*Steady* is the supporter who works well with others. Probably the biggest fault with the steady personality is the lack of decisiveness. Since the high "S" usually gets along well with almost any other personality, this is one of the rare cases where two similar types may get married. Their conversations often go like this:

> "Where do you want to eat?"
> "Oh, I don't care. You decide."
> "Well, I don't care either. You decide."
> "No, you decide."

It will continue like this until they have a strong-willed "D" child who will dominate their lives if they don't take control.

*Conscientious* is the perfectionist who wants clear-cut guidelines and conformance to detail. You'll know him when he orders the swing set, because before he begins he will not only read the instructions but also correct the spelling and grammar.

Obviously, there will be differences of opinion when two different personalities are placed in the close proximity that a marriage creates. But differences don't necessarily have to lead to conflicts.

God's Word says, "For this reason a man shall leave his father and his mother, and be joined to his wife; and they shall become one flesh" (Gen. 2:24). In other words, a married couple becomes one person. Two personalities merge in a marriage to operate as one. The extremes of one person are balanced by the partner's extremes.

Quite often, single people live lives of extremes. They are frequently classic examples of imbalanced lifestyles. And even within the same family, their personalities are totally different. My wife and I raised four children—all different.

When our oldest son was growing up, you could go into his room and know exactly what he was like. It was clean; his bed was made; the books were in order on his desk. If you went into our other son's room, you had to carry a stick with you because there were things that lived under his bed.

Our oldest son is now married and has four children. He still straightens some, but he's learned to relax and tolerate some clutter. His wife is an excellent balance to his personality because she is as outgoing as he is shy.

If sloppy singles never got married, they would have to buy new clothes continually because they would never wash the old ones! Without balance and accountability, extremes are the norm. A Bible-based marriage is two people willing to merge their lives totally as partners to utilize their strengths. That's called balance, and that's what a marriage should be. In the area of finances, balance is especially critical. "An excellent wife, who can find? For her worth is far above jewels. The heart of her husband trusts in her, and he will have no lack of gain" (Prov. 31:10–11).

# 4   GOD'S MINIMUM STANDARDS

God's Word provides standards for managing money that are essential for marital unity. One of the things I find in counseling couples, both married and premarried, is that whatever I might convince them to do, somebody else coming along behind me could convince them otherwise. So I decided a long time ago that I would stop trying to convince them to do anything. Instead I would go back to the source of truth, God's Word, and let God do the convincing.

God requires minimum standards of us as Christians. If you, as husband and wife, will establish the standards that God's Word establishes, you will come out with a healthy, balanced marriage.

## STANDARD NUMBER 1: GOD OWNS EVERYTHING

As Paul wrote to Timothy, "For we have brought nothing into the world, so we cannot take anything out of it either" (1 Tim. 6:7). Once you accept the fact that God owns everything, it's important to manage all you have according to His rules. It's how you manage money that determines how you will manage greater things. For instance, unless you surrender to each other your rights over money, you will not surrender other rights. The question is this: Isn't it worth sacrificing some short-term indulgences to establish long-term peace in a marriage?

Perhaps the situation I have seen that best demonstrates this principle is where a wife either brings financial assets into a marriage or earns her own money through a job. If she truly believes that a husband and wife are to be one and that all that she has belongs to God, she will withhold nothing in the marriage relationship. They will merge their assets and operate from a unified base.

However, if ego or fear of the future takes over, she will resist a total merger and maintain a degree of independence. This is the first wedge Satan uses to ultimately split one back into two. It's a self-first attitude, rather than God-first. Obviously, the same principle applies to the husband's assets and income. As Proverb 14:12 says, "There is a way which seems right to a man, but its end is the way of death."

## STANDARD NUMBER 2: THINK AHEAD AND AVOID PROBLEMS

The Lord taught His disciples, "For which one of you, when he wants to build a tower, does not first sit down and calculate the cost to see if he has enough to complete it?" (Luke 14:28). Too often, young couples put off planning until they're in trouble. Then it's usually too late, except for "crisis" planning.

I recommend that you write down your goals and objectives before you're married, including a first year's budget. Then every year, plan to go away somewhere together for at least one day just to update your budget and evaluate your goals. If you will make this a priority, it will be the best investment of time you'll ever make.

Obviously, your minimum goal should be to avoid financial bondage through debt. This doesn't mean you can't borrow to buy anything. But borrowing to buy consumables such as gifts, vacations, even cars will put a family in bondage quickly. Buying something on credit that you can't afford doesn't take into consideration the decision that you shouldn't buy it; credit only delays the consequences and makes them worse.

I can remember at Christmas seeing a large billboard produced by a credit card company that said, "Go ahead and do it. You owe it to yourself." Let me assure you, they didn't mean that. What they really meant was, "Go ahead and do it, and you'll owe it to us at 21 percent per year."

Remember standard number 2: think ahead.

## STANDARD NUMBER 3: KEEP GOOD RECORDS

In counseling young couples, I discovered that less than two out of ten knew how to balance a checkbook. Solomon wrote, "By wisdom a house is built, and by understanding it is established; and by knowledge the rooms are filled with all precious and pleasant riches" (Prov. 24:3–4). It is impossible to have your finances under control without understanding the basics of good bookkeeping. Very few young couples understand how to evaluate life insurance, how much to spend on housing, what car they can afford, or how to work a baby into their budget. But even worse, often they don't know how much they are spending.

In the majority of marriages, the wife ends up being the bookkeeper. She's the one who is usually responsible for keeping the books balanced, writing the checks, and paying the bills. That doesn't mean that the husband should not be involved; he should, and he must be. A couple should develop their plans together and work together. But there can be only *one* bookkeeper in the home. When there are two bookkeepers, you'll have two messes.

Typically, in more than 80 percent of the families we counsel, the wife is the bookkeeper. Usually the wife has more time and pays more attention to detail. Therefore, she makes the better bookkeeper. But in order to do it well, she must know how to do it. Later I'll discuss how to balance a checkbook and how to develop a budget. But for now, take my word that unless you do, you won't have peace in your marriage.

## STANDARD NUMBER 4: GET EDUCATED

"The naive believes everything, but the sensible man considers his steps" (Prov. 14:15). Most naive people are ignorant. Ignorant does not mean stupid; it means unknowledgeable. For instance, many couples borrow money without understanding the actual interest rate. Their primary concern at the time is, "How much are the monthly payments?" Others borrow more money than they can repay because they have no system of budgeting. They truly don't know where their money goes each month or how much credit their income can support.

I once assumed that almost everyone knew how to balance a checking account. I quickly discovered that was an erroneous assumption. Many people have only a vague idea of how much is in their bank accounts and have never balanced their accounts. They write checks and fail to record them in their ledger, they pay overdraft charges on checks written on insufficient funds, and they simply accept the bank's statement as totally accurate.

One couple—Craig and Cathy—was even paying for the bank's errors. Cathy kept the "books" for their home records. After our first session, I had a strong suspicion that the books weren't being kept too well, as Craig and Cathy regularly paid overdraft charges for insufficient funds. So I asked Cathy to bring her bank statement and ledger book the next visit. A month passed before we talked again, and during that time two more checks bounced. I asked Cathy how she balanced her checkbook after she received the monthly bank statement. "Oh, I look to be sure that every check they return is really ours."

"Good, no problem there," I said.

"Next, I cross off all the returned checks in my checkbook." (No problem there either, except that she forgot to mention she couldn't find all of them in her checkbook.) "Then I subtract the service charge and overdraft charges from my checkbook, deduct my outstanding checks from the bank's account, and compare my checkbook to their statement."

"Great," I said. "How do they compare?"

"Oh, they never do," replied Cathy. "So I always use the bank's figure."

I discovered two things about this method of home accounting: (1) it is a very common method of keeping records; (2) it is grossly inaccurate.

Cathy had some enormous problems in her records. Because she didn't write down every check, she obviously couldn't subtract them from the bank's balance. Thus, there always seemed to be more money than there really was. We also discovered that the bank had actually paid the returned checks the first time through, added an insufficient funds penalty, and returned the check to the payee, who then resubmitted the check. By that time, there were additional funds in the account and the check cleared, but Cathy's account was again debited the amount of the check.

So she had actually paid the checks twice, plus penalties. When we researched the bank account, we were able to recover over $200 in overpayments during the previous year. Through this lesson, Cathy became a knowledgeable home record keeper. She now helps teach other women how to manage their home accounts.

I've counseled enough to know the simplest economic principle ever written is, "If you don't overspend, you won't get in debt." And I have never counseled a couple who purposely set out to get themselves into debt. They usually let their record keeping get so bad that they had no idea where they were financially. Then they would call and say, "We've got a disaster. The creditors are going to repossess our car [or our home or our child]," or whatever their particular disaster was.

As you probably know, it's a lot of fun to get into debt, but it's not nearly as much fun to get out of debt. Learn what you need to know, and use that information to avoid financial problems.

# 5   HOW GOD USES MONEY IN A MARRIAGE

As I said earlier, God uses money in a Christian marriage to show us our strengths and weaknesses and to teach us to depend on Him more fully.

## A TEST OF FAITHFULNESS

One way God uses money is to test our faithfulness. Remember, the way we handle money is an outside expression of what's going on in our lives spiritually. The way we respond to financial problems is a good indicator of whether we trust God or whether we just say we trust God. In other words, when the pressure's on, will we still do it God's way?

John and Paula had been married about five years when I met them. They were both Christians, members of a sound denominational church, and faithful in their giving to God's work. They had wanted to have children soon after their marriage and always budgeted based on John's income so that Paula could stay home when they had their first child.

Paula had gotten pregnant twice, but she miscarried both times. During the third pregnancy she was told to go to bed and rest from the third month on. She carried the baby full term and delivered without any major problems. However, shortly after the baby was born, Paula was diagnosed with leukemia. While she was undergoing therapy, John lost his job when the company he worked for shut down. The bills piled up, both personal and medical, until their lives became strained to the breaking point.

When they came to see me, they owed over $40,000 in personal bills. The utility company was threatening to shut off their power, the phone was disconnected, and they were two months behind in rent.

After reviewing their situation, I could see no way to resolve their financial problems. An attorney for their creditors had suggested that they file for bankruptcy because it was apparent they would never be able to pay their bills. My question to John and Paula was the same one that God asks each of us: "Do you trust God?" It's easy to say you trust God when things are going well, but the bottom line is, do you *really* trust God? As Shadrach, Meshach, and Abed-nego said, "Our God whom we serve is able to deliver us from the furnace of blazing fire; and He will deliver us out of your hand, O king. But even if He does not, let it be known to you, O king, that we are not going to serve your gods or worship the golden image that you have set up" (Dan. 3:17–18). Can you still trust God, even though you can see no logical way out?

John and Paula said they did trust God and knew inside that they should not go bankrupt. They left with a commitment to take their needs back to their church and ask for the church's help.

In the meantime, I mentioned their need at a men's Bible study I taught. One of the men at our study knew of another Christian who was looking for an employee with John's qualifications. It turned out that John was an answer to his very specific prayers for a loyal, hardworking Christian to help in his business. In addition, two of our group took on the task of raising some of the needed funds to clear the immediate debts. The results were beyond our imaginations as other churches and Sunday school classes took up the challenge. Within two weeks, our group, along with John and Paula's church, had raised over $40,000 and all the bills were paid—in full. God had honored their commitment to trust Him and taught us a lesson as well: God had provided what they needed already—through us.

## SOME ARE CHEAP

Not every couple is going to have debt problems. A small percentage of our population is basically so cheap (or frugal) that these individuals are never going to get into debt. I, for example, will never knowingly get into debt. There's some control system inside me that keeps me from overspending. I can't stand to pay interest and I can't stand to owe anyone, so if I borrow, it's short term and very limited.

## SOME ARE SLOPPY

Another small segment of our population makes enough money to be sloppy and get away with it. They feel they can live without a budget because if they should get into financial trouble, they can simply cut back on their indulgences for a while and pay their way out of it. Very few young couples fit into this category. Usually these "sloppies" are the attorneys, dentists, and doctors among us. Most doctors, for instance, make far more than the national average, so you might think they don't have financial problems. That's not true. They're the classic example that it's not what you make that's important but how much you spend.

I was working in my office one afternoon when an attorney friend called to ask for some counsel. It seems that a client of his, a doctor, had been served notice by the IRS that his property was being attached (legally taken over) for failure to pay taxes. In fact, this doctor had arrived home one evening to find an IRS agent there impounding his cars, home, and furnishings. He rushed to the attorney's office, and the attorney then called me. Sadly, this was not the first such episode of financial woes for the doctor, and the attorney realized that a pattern was developing. I suggested that the doctor and his wife come in for counsel.

It turned out that this doctor had used some of his employees' withholding tax funds to invest in a great "deal" being touted by another Christian. He forgot about using the tax money and didn't pay his quarterly withholding. However, the IRS didn't forget, and when several notices failed to get a response, the agency attached his assets.

A little negotiating got the attachments lifted, and the doctor started paying monthly to clear the back taxes. He did well for about three months. Then a friend offered him a great buy on a sailboat (to make a quick profit). Lacking the necessary funds, he again dipped into his tax funds. He intended to pay the money back out of his quick profits. This idea of quick profit is known as "the greater sucker theory." In other words, if you're sucker enough to buy it, there must be a greater sucker than you around who will pay a higher price.

Well, the boat didn't sell and he missed another tax payment. This time the IRS attached everything, even his checking accounts. He couldn't even write a check for groceries. He was physically ill when he called to ask for help. On the way to my office, he told his wife, "Whatever he tells me to do, I'm going to do it. I swear to God."

Incidentally, this might be a good time to mention Solomon's words in Ecclesiastes 5:4: "When you make a vow to God, do not be late in paying it; for He takes no delight in fools. Pay what you vow!" So be careful about urgent vows or you might get stuck with them.

I didn't know about the doctor's vow, but I did have a plan in mind that his attorney and I had discussed. He walked in, ghost white and quite obviously under great stress. The IRS agent had mentioned "fraud" and "prosecution," which are terms that strike fear in the hearts of virtually every taxpayer.

I shared a story with him that I believed would fit his situation perfectly. I asked, "Would you agree that your problem is not a lack of money?"

He responded, "I suppose not." That point was made clear in previous counseling sessions when he discussed increasing his office hours to make more money. His annual income was about $180,000.

"Are you familiar with the story in 2 Kings about an Assyrian army captain by the name of Naaman who went to Israel to be healed of leprosy?" I asked. He said he had heard the story before. So I continued. Naaman heard there was a prophet in Israel who served the true God and could heal even lepers. So he headed toward Israel with his troops. But instead of going out to meet the captain, Elisha sent a messenger to tell Naaman to go down to the Jordan River, dunk himself seven times, and his flesh would be restored.

Naaman was furious and stormed away, saying, "Behold, I thought, 'He will surely come out to me and stand and call on the name of the LORD his God, and wave his hand over the place and cure the leper.'" Then one of his servants asked him, "My father, had the prophet told you to do some great thing, would you not have done it?" And of course

Naaman said yes. Then the servant said, "How much more then, when he says to you, 'Wash, and be clean'?" And so Naaman went down to the river, dunked himself seven times, and when he came up the seventh time, his leprosy was gone (2 Kings 5:1–14).

I concluded, "The principle behind this story is that God works best with a humble spirit." What I then asked the doctor to do was mow lawns on his day off (Wednesdays) until he had paid off the smallest of his debts (about $160).

"That's stupid. I'm not going to do that," he retorted. "I'm a radiologist. I can make more than that in one hour."

I reminded him, "What you make is not the issue here. It's what you spend. But you don't have to do it. It's just a suggestion." He looked at his wife as if to say, "How did you tell him what I said without me knowing about it?" Then he stormed out of my office with his wife in tow.

She waited until they were nearly home before she said, "Are you going to do what you promised God?" He stomped around the house for a few days while his attorney was working out an ironclad plan to get the IRS paid back. Then he came to his wife and said, "I'll do it. It's stupid, but I gave my word and I'll do it."

It was several weeks before I saw them again and heard what happened. "The first week I set out to get some jobs mowing lawns, I realized I was in trouble," he said. "I found myself in competition with twelve-year-old kids, so I told my neighbors I needed exercise but also needed the money as an incentive. I figured they didn't buy it when we started finding care packages on our doorstep. But I stuck it out even though I was down to two bucks a lawn sometimes. Finally, I paid that bill off, and I felt like I had been released from prison.

Then I realized what an impact it had made on me. One day I was driving around and saw a Greyhound bus that had been converted into a motor home. Man, I have always wanted one of those motor homes. But you know what stopped me? Just thinking about mowing lawns to pay off a $66,000 motor home," he explained.

If you happen to be among that fortunate 10 percent who make a significant income—and some of you will be, at some point—remember it's *not* what you make that generates debt. It's what you spend.

## THE AVERAGE SPENDER

The remaining members of the population are not frugal enough to stay out of debt, nor do they make enough money to buy their way out of trouble. These families represent the norm. Although everybody *should* live on a budget, this group *must* live on a budget or risk getting deeply into debt. Easy credit is one of the most subtle traps Satan lays for Christian families. God's Word says watch out: "The prudent sees the evil and hides himself, but the naive go on, and are punished for it" (Prov. 22:3).

Again, let me make the point here that borrowing itself is *not* a problem. If used prudently, some credit is reasonable. Even when somebody borrows so much that he or she can't pay it back, it's not really a financial problem. It's a symptom of a spiritual problem. The real problem is a lack of trust in God. If we trust God, He will provide all we need within our income, which leads me to the next principle.

## DOES GOD REALLY LOVE US?

Another way that God uses money is to demonstrate that He really does love us. I think of what Jesus said: "What man is there among you who, when his son asks for a loaf, will give him a stone? Or if he asks for a fish, he will not give him a snake, will he? If you then, being evil, know how to give good gifts to your children, how much more will your Father who is in heaven give what is good to those who ask Him!" (Matt. 7:9–11). There are three prerequisites for receiving God's best:

1. Love and trust Him as your personal Savior.
2. Be willing to obey Him.
3. Demonstrate this obedience by following His principles.

God is going to bless those who are willing to say, "God, we trust You, and since You know best, maybe we can do without that five-bedroom, three-bath home that we think we need. We're willing to be content with a two-bedroom, one-bath apartment for a while believing that, somewhere down the road, You have exactly the right home that we can afford within our budget."

It boils down to a set of decisions.

1. Do you really trust God?
2. Are you willing to put that trust into action?
3. Are you willing to wait upon God's provision?

## A COMMUNICATIONS TOOL

God uses money in the lives of any young couple to draw them closer together. In contrast, Satan wants to drive a wedge between a husband and wife. Why? In hopes that the resultant turmoil will drive them away from God.

God will bring you closer together if, from the very beginning, you will establish God's Word as your financial guide. That means, in a practical sense, that you must decide what kind of home you can afford, what kind of car you can buy, what kind of vacation you can take, how much you can spend on clothes, entertainment, recreation, and so forth. And you must commit to making all those decisions *together*.

As you begin to communicate about these everyday things, you'll learn a lot about each other. Keep in mind that you're almost always going to approach things from different perspectives. As I said earlier, if two people are identical, one is unnecessary. Differences can be a source of argument, or they can be a source of positive balance. When a couple accepts this principle, both the husband and wife realize that each of them has strengths and weaknesses.

A friend of mine, who is a Christian psychologist, shared that he and his wife are opposites, and for a long time it caused a lot of strife. He said, "I know that whatever I want to do, she'll want to do the opposite. Whatever I want to buy, she wants to buy something else. If I say black, she says white." But, he said, he knew how to get to her. She was sensitive about her lack of education, because he had a PhD. So he would berate her lack of education during an argument. But what used to irritate him, he said, was that with a high school education, she would consistently give better advice than he would with his PhD.

He said that before they became Christians they used to get into terrible fights—usually after she had bruised his ego. Then they both became Christians and he thought surely their problems were solved, especially when he learned about the submission principle for wives (which he referred to a lot).

Then one time he was asked to speak at a pastors' conference, and his wife was asked to speak to the women while he spoke to the men. Despite his badgering, she refused to discuss what she was going to talk about. He said, "I knew she was going to blow my image." Then one day he saw a note she had scribbled while obviously working on her presentation. It read, "Life with Attila the Hun." He was so mad that by the time they left for the conference he wasn't speaking anymore. He drove for a couple of hours with neither of them saying a word, then got off the freeway to get some gas. He filled the tank, paid for the gas, and headed down the freeway again.

The first words his wife spoke were, "Do you know you're headed in the wrong direction?"

He said, "Boy, did that make me mad. So I asked her, 'Don't you think that with a PhD I've got enough sense to know which way to go?'" As he drove on, he quickly realized he was going in the wrong direction. But he drove on thirty minutes more, wondering, *How can I turn this car around without her realizing it?*

After that, he grasped God's plan in his marriage—balance. Together they functioned pretty well. Apart, they looked pretty foolish—especially him.

He told me they still don't agree on everything. "But that's okay," he said, "because now we realize we're not supposed to." By communicating even their differences, they are able to reach a better decision than either can independently. "Now when we discuss something," he said, "do you know what I find? My best is her worst and her best is my worst. But somewhere in between, we always find a point we can agree on. As a result, we have become much closer. We have learned that neither of us is ever totally right. Now we have communication, not combat."

## WHO IS THE SPENDTHRIFT?

Let me correct a common misconception made in most marriages. The majority of spending in a marriage is *not* done by the wife. Under an impulse, a woman will buy too much food or too many clothes. Under the same impulse, her husband will buy a new car, a motorcycle, or a large entertainment system. We men may not buy often, but when we do, we buy big-ticket items. The majority of indebtedness in most marriages comes as a result of the husband's spending.

Husbands, I would suggest some simple impulse-buying rules. First, don't ever buy anything that isn't budgeted, unless you wait at least thirty days. Second, get at least three different prices on the item within that thirty days. Third, never have more than one item on your impulse list at any time. Do you know what you'll find if you do this? You won't buy on impulse, because first, before the thirty days are up, you'll find something else you want more than the first item. So you'll scratch the first item off and add your new item. Then you'll have to wait another thirty days, and the impulse will pass (usually).

In summary, I encourage Christian couples to accept the fact that unless you communicate about your finances, you can never achieve oneness, because money is the one subject that's going to occupy the majority of your time.

# 6   CREDIT CARDS

There are a lot of myths about credit that young couples need to understand. The first is that you must have credit in our society. Don't misunderstand. There is nothing unbiblical about borrowing money. Scripture does not prohibit borrowing. But there is not one positive reference to borrowing money in all of the Bible. All references to borrowing are negative. Most of them are warnings. For instance, according to Proverbs 22:7, "The rich rules over the poor, and the borrower becomes the lender's slave." I would encourage every young couple to memorize that proverb and believe it. It is all too easy in our society to be in bondage to lenders.

## DO YOU NEED CREDIT?

Many young couples ask, "How can we establish credit?" The first thing I try to convince them is this: don't establish credit unless you have a specific purpose for it and you know how to use it wisely. I believe that every credit card should have this warning

### DANGER! USE OF THIS CARD CAN BE INJURIOUS TO YOUR MARRIAGE

printed on the face of it. Perhaps you think you can handle credit. So did every couple who ever got into debt. Rarely does anyone set out to get into debt. Virtually every couple I ever counseled who was in debt said the same thing: "How in the world did we get into a mess like this?"

Drew and Nan were seemingly the ideal couple. They both graduated from college on the dean's list. Drew went on to law school; Nan took a teaching position.

After law school, Drew joined a law firm headed by Nan's father. Everyone assumed their large home was provided by their well-to-do parents. But in reality it was provided by extending themselves far beyond their income. As creditors began to press them, Drew began to speculate in stocks, trying desperately to hit the "big one" and get out of debt. He knew that any open publicity about their financial troubles would severely injure his career.

Nan was totally ignorant of their finances and took Drew's word that their lifestyle was supported by bonuses from the law firm. In actuality, Drew was taking money systematically from clients' trust accounts, which he was managing. The final blow came with a bank-directed audit of the trust accounts. When the audit was completed, it revealed a $64,000 deficit in client trust funds. Drew was disbarred from practicing law and served three years in a federal prison—all because of a desire by him and his wife to live beyond their means.

Drew didn't consider himself dishonest. He always intended to repay the accounts and kept detailed records of what he "borrowed." Many other couples have faced similar situations, only they have borrowed from friends, family, and creditors. Their defaults were considered legal because they filed bankruptcy. Yet the emotional and spiritual consequences were very similar.

Lenders promote the idea that you should establish credit early. Obviously so; that's how they earn their living. But the longer you can go without credit (and credit cards), the less you will depend on it later. Whatever you do, don't use credit for consumable items such as clothes, food, vacations, or repairs. We're the only generation in history to borrow significant amounts of money to buy consumables. Our grandparents didn't borrow the way we do. They lived on what they earned, saved, and then bought. Today, it's "buy and pay later." Unfortunately, sometimes couples buy beyond their ability to repay.

## CAN CREDIT CARDS BE USED WISELY?

Another common myth is that credit cards can be used wisely. Don't be deceived. They can be used less foolishly, but rarely, if ever, wisely. Credit cards are not problems, but they certainly can lead to problems. A credit card, if managed properly, can be useful. But virtually everyone will buy more using a credit card than if he or she used only cash. I've heard people say, "I pay mine off every month," implying that they use it wisely. Quite often, that's simply not true. I'm a very budget-conscious person, as I shared earlier, and I do use credit cards when I travel. I pay mine off every month and have never paid any interest on them. And yet, if I'm not careful, I will spend more using those plastic cards than if I use only cash.

About twelve years ago, I got rid of my credit cards and went without them for nearly ten years. The reason was because the majority of people I was counseling had misused credit, and when I would ask them to get rid of their credit cards, the first thing they would ask is, "Do you use them?"

I had to say, "Yes, I do, but I use mine wisely."

Then they would say, "Well, from now on, I promise to handle mine properly too." But they seldom did.

So I decided to get rid of my credit cards to see if I could travel without them. I did so for the better part of ten years. Do you know what I found out? I wasn't nearly as conservative as I thought, because I had been buying things with credit cards that I would never have bought with cash. At airports I would often buy something because I could pay for it thirty days later. Or I would eat at a more expensive restaurant because I didn't have to pay for it in cash. Many times I would stay at a hotel or motel where I would not have stayed if I had to put out the money in cash. Remember, you can use credit cards less foolishly, but you rarely use a credit card wisely. That's a common myth.

However, if you are going to use credit cards, as most couples will, establish some fundamental rules and stick to them. I would suggest three basic rules:

1. Use your credit cards only for *budgeted* items. In other words, if it's not in your budget for the month, don't buy it on credit.

2. Pay your credit cards off *every* month. Never pay interest at credit card rates, which are usurious.

3. The first month that you find you cannot pay off your credit card bills, *destroy* your credit cards and don't ever get any more.

If you follow these basic rules, credit cards won't become a source of financial bondage to you.

## IS INTEREST A GOOD TAX BREAK?

Another common myth in our generation is that somehow interest is a good tax break. Let me illustrate why this isn't true. Let's assume you're in a 25 percent tax bracket and you pay $1,000 a year in interest. Let's further assume you can claim the interest as a deduction against your income tax. The government will return $250 of your tax dollars, right? What happened to the other $750? As best I can tell, you lost it.

Let me make you a much better deal than that. If you'll give me $1,000, I'll give you back $900. So all it will cost you is $100 to give me $1,000. Isn't that a better deal? Of course it is, for me—just as the interest you pay is a better deal for the lender.

Paying interest is always a loss, and you need to be sure you're not duped into thinking that somehow that's a good deal. It is not. Interest is still money out of your pocket, and unless you're in a tax bracket of more than 100 percent, you'll have a loss on every dollar paid. As Proverbs 14:18 says, "The naive inherit foolishness, but the sensible are crowned with knowledge."

# 7   EARLY MARRIAGE SYMPTOMS

Next I'd like to discuss the differences between symptoms and problems. Many young couples suffer financial symptoms, but remember that the symptom is only what you see on the outside. If you deal only with what you see, the problem will crop up somewhere else. You must deal with the source to correct the problem.

Why do people want to deal with symptoms rather than problems? Because relieving the symptom provides fast, temporary peace. Unfortunately, when the next symptom appears, it is usually worse than the previous one and more difficult to deal with.

Let's look at some escape mechanisms many husbands and wives use in futile attempts to ease the pain of financial troubles.

## AVOIDING REALITY

One way to relieve tension temporarily is to pretend that no problem exists. Most people who avoid reality simply seek to postpone the inevitable.

Businesspeople have been known to manipulate every conceivable angle in an attempt to prolong the life of a hopeless business even one more day. Had they been asked to counsel other businesspeople in similar situations, often they would have advised them to shut down and liquidate earlier.

Why do people refuse to face the reality of a situation sooner? The answer is that they hope some miracle will reverse the situation and bail them out.

I believe in miracles. But I have observed that God does not violate His scriptural principles to accomplish His goals; He always follows His own rules.

## LITTLE WHITE LIES

A common symptom is for one spouse to lie to the other about their financial situation just as the attorney, Drew, did in our earlier example. It may be an effort to ignore the problems, or it may be fear of conflict. This is especially true of husbands. They are more likely to deceive their spouses if they are suffering marital problems, including financial ones. In the process of trying to hide all traces of the true situation, they may borrow additional money to keep up the front, including tapping every close friend or relative.

Unfortunately, this ruse cannot be maintained forever, and eventually the truth will be known. It may be the creditors or a series of snide comments by friends or family, but eventually the facts will surface.

When a wife has been deceived and learns the truth from a source other than her husband, the results are predictable. First, she is hurt and offended that seemingly everybody knew the truth but her. Then, she is distrustful because she wonders what else has been kept from her. In her eyes, her position in the family has been downgraded because her husband has no confidence in her. Soon, many other areas of their relationship will be questioned and an air of distrust will be generated.

## GET AWAY FROM IT ALL

Just as many people under the pressures of financial problems buy new cars and boats to lift their spirits, many families seek to escape their present symptoms.

When finances really get tight, one of the common tendencies is to take a vacation. The logic is simple: retreat into something that will be remembered as a happy experience. On vacation, troubles are temporarily left behind. Unfortunately, those who try to avoid facing reality in this manner quickly discover that a vacation under stress is no different from a job under stress. By the time the trip is over, the symptoms are even worse.

The ultimate escape for many families is to quit their jobs and move to another area for a fresh start. Just as in the previous circumstance, this will not help. This get-away-from-it-all urge needs to be controlled and the situation faced squarely and honestly.

## BILL CONSOLIDATION LOAN

A family that piles up debts from many areas—credit cards, bank loans, and finance company loans—is faced with a choice: stop the flow of credit and reduce spending to pay off the debts, or look for new sources of money.

One of these sources is called a *bill consolidation loan*. The purpose is to combine several small debts into one large loan so that the payments can be spread over a longer period of time, thus reducing the monthly outgo. Most finance companies encourage such loans, especially when one of *their* existing loans will be refinanced. Why? Because the amount refinanced includes not only principal but some of the interest as well, so they actually earn interest on the interest.

The logic behind this kind of symptom treatment sounds reasonable. It does reduce the monthly payments in most cases. When many of the debts are on credit cards, it may actually reduce the interest paid. But bill consolidation treats a symptom, not the problem. The symptom here is a lack of money on a month-by-month basis. The problem is overspending. Unless the overspending is stopped first, the symptom of debt will return in a few months, resulting in even worse problems. The family will be trapped with all the small debts again, as well as the consolidation loan.

One advantage of bill consolidation loans is to provide extra cash. In other words, the finance company will consolidate the bills and also extend the loan to give some surplus money. Unfortunately, this only amplifies the original problem.

Often a family will use the surplus as a down payment on a large purchase (thereby incurring more debt) or put it aside as a buffer to use on monthly overspending. By the time the surplus is gone, they have adjusted spending to a higher level and have become dependent on it. Rather than adjust the spending down, they substitute credit-card spending.

A couple I'll call Don and Ann would have been classified as a typical young couple when they got married. They both came from middle-income Christian parents who loved them and indulged them, as most parents do today. As children, they both had chores to do and allowances that provided them with ample spending money. Later they both worked summer jobs for additional spending money to buy extras like records, tapes, and designer clothes. Their parents provided them with the use of the family cars in high school and later bought them cars of their own.

Without realizing it, Don's and Ann's parents were acclimating them to a lifestyle they couldn't maintain on their own. Like most young couples, they tried to duplicate what their parents had, and more. At first they rented an apartment, but in less than six months they decided that apartment living was not for them. Their decision to move was cemented when a couple of young single guys moved into the apartment next to them, hung six-foot speakers on the wall adjacent to their apartment, and played loud music all night. Pretty soon they said, "We can't stand this apartment. We need a home." So they went looking for a house.

Don and Ann made a common mistake that many young couples make. They looked at four-bedroom, two-bath houses first. Once they saw them, they knew they could never be satisfied with a two-bedroom, one-bath home. They realized that the house they wanted was out of their price range, but the less expensive homes were in less desirable neighborhoods. At the same time, both sets of parents realized they couldn't let their kids get stuck with run-down housing, so they encouraged them to look in the "better" areas.

With this kind of parental guidance, they just knew God was telling them to trust Him. They couldn't qualify to buy a home because they didn't have the down payment. So one parent loaned them $10,000 for the down payment on a $90,000 home. They tried to finance an $80,000 mortgage but couldn't qualify for that either, so the builder, a friend of the family, agreed to carry a second mortgage for $15,000. With their mortgage down to $65,000, they finally qualified. It took about 60 percent of their total income to pay the payments, interest, and taxes.

Each month they struggled to make the mortgage payments, and they had to let other expenses back up. In about a year they found themselves deeply in debt. They couldn't even afford to keep their old car repaired since it took nearly $75 a month to keep it running. So they bought a new car at $275 a month. In another six months, they couldn't keep their mortgage payments current. There was not enough money to buy even the essentials. Since there seemed to be no other choice at that point, Ann decided she had to go to work. They were certain that more income would be the solution.

Their income increased a little, but their expenses increased even more. There was more eating out, more clothes, another car. Within another year, they had consumed her salary and were deeper in debt than ever before.

It is at this point where most couples decide to consolidate their bills. They even made payments to their parents for a few months. With the pressures of the delinquent bills relieved, they assumed the problems were solved. Not so. With a house payment too high for their budget and two car loans, they fell right back into the same spending habits and, within a year, they had all of the little bills back again *plus* the consolidation loan.

By this time, they were having daily arguments about money, and Ann was feeling great anxiety as they drifted deeper into debt. Their Bible study and their prayer time together were nonexistent. They didn't talk anymore. They argued about virtually everything, even nonfinancial matters. Creditors pressured Ann at home and at work with phone calls and certified collection letters. Usually creditors attempt to contact the wife, if possible, because they know if they pressure her, she'll pressure her husband.

If not corrected quickly, such a financial nightmare situation can lead to severe marriage problems. In Don and Ann's case, it led to a divorce that neither one ever thought could happen. Their mistake of buying too expensive a home was compounded by treating only the symptoms it created. Most couples can avoid these consequences, but only if they decide to deal with the problems rather than simply treat the symptoms.

For instance, if a young couple spends more than they make, often they will ask their parents for help. Parents don't want their children to be under pressure so, with good intentions, they give or lend the kids money. Does that solve the problem? No. It treats the symptom. The problem will surface again elsewhere.

Until husbands and wives learn to manage the money they already have, more money will not help. God's Word teaches elementary principles of self-discipline. Most young couples have been taught to think the world's way. Now you must condition yourself to think God's way. Manage well what you have before looking for more.

# 8   CORRECTING THE PROBLEMS

The real problems surrounding finances are usually related to one of three basic areas: ignorance, greed, and communication. Let's look at the first problem: ignorance.

# IGNORANCE

Ignorance is not stupidity. Ignorance is a lack of understanding. For example, I received a call one afternoon from a young man who sounded very desperate. He said, "I have an urgent problem. My wife, Melody, has been arrested for writing a bad check, and they put her in jail. Can you help us?"

The first thing we did was arrange for someone to go to the jail and bail her out. When they both came in for counseling the next day, I asked Melody, "Why did you write a bad check? Did you do it purposely?"

"No," she said, "I don't understand it. I was sure I had enough money in my account to pay all of my bills."

It turned out this was the *third* time Melody had written the same merchant a bad check. That's why she was arrested. I asked to see her checkbook, which she then handed over. Even an accountant could not have balanced that checkbook! Apparently, being a courteous woman, she didn't want to keep anybody waiting in line while she wrote down the amount of her purchase, so she normally waited until she got home to record her checks. Sometimes she waited as long as a week or so to write them down. Anyone who has ever done this realizes that by that time, it's hard to remember whether a check was for $16.11 or $11.16, so Melody just wrote down something close. Usually she would write a question mark next to the amount of the check. Occasionally the amount would be scratched out with a note beside it. For instance, "See check No. 62." So I turned to check No. 62, which referenced check No. 61, which referenced check No. 59, and so on.

"My goodness, do you ever balance your checkbook?" I wondered aloud.

By this time she was crying when she said, "I try, every single month." So I asked her to explain how she balanced it. "Well, the first thing I do is look through all of my checks to be sure that I actually wrote them. In other words, that they're my check images and not somebody else's." There's certainly nothing wrong with that. "Then," she continued, "I take the amounts of my checks and compare them with the amounts in my checkbook, and I correct it."

"Well, that's not the best method, but it's understandable. Then what do you do?"

"I look at my statement online. It tells me how much money I have left in my account. Then I add that to my checkbook, and I can write some more checks."

I said, "No, I don't believe it works that way. You went through two steps of balancing a checkbook. But there are seven more steps." I spent the next thirty minutes teaching her how to balance her checkbook; then she understood her mistakes. (Note: You will find the same procedure in appendix A of this book.) We made only two other changes. First, she closed out her old account and opened a new one (no one could figure out how much was actually in the old account). Second, I had her start using a checkbook that provided a duplicate copy of every check written, so the amount was always certain. From that point on, she always balanced her account properly every month. This was not a stupid woman. She was a high school math teacher with a graduate degree. She was intelligent, but ignorant. As Proverbs 27:23 says, "Know well the condition of your flocks, and pay attention to your herds." In other words, know what you're doing!

# GREED

The second source of financial problems is greed. What does greed mean? You have to have more, and you have to have the best. Today greed is accepted as normal. In our generation, it's taught under the guise that you owe it to yourself, or you buy it because somebody else has one too. The only way to overcome that philosophy is to ask, "What is God's plan for me? I don't want somebody else's plan."

Perhaps God wants you to live in an apartment complex for a while so that you can witness to people there. After all, God has to have His people stationed in apartment complexes around the country, doesn't He?

I think of a young couple I'll call Ben and Mary who made a conscious decision to live God's plan for their lives and not someone else's. Ben was an engineer with an MBA from Harvard. Mary was the only daughter of a very wealthy family. They were living in an affluent section of their city, with the best of what the world has to offer, when Ben felt strongly that God wanted them to move to a transitional neighborhood in the inner city.

Both of their families tried to talk them out of moving. But they were certain that they were supposed to have a ministry in an area that most middle-class families had abandoned. Within a year they had sold their BMW, Ben had quit his engineering job, and he was working with an inner-city planning commission.

During the next five years, Ben and Mary were responsible for organizing other middle- and upper-income families to raise funds for urban renewal. To date, they have refurbished over one hundred run-down homes with totally private funds and have given or sold them (at no interest) to low-income families, particularly elderly people. Because Ben and Mary chose to live God's plan for their lives, several city officials came to know Jesus Christ as Savior and have become staunch allies of Christianity, to which they were openly hostile previously.

Perhaps God wants to teach us to trust Him, or perhaps He wants us to get along without all the trinkets and toys our generation strives after. At some point, every couple has to ask, "What is God's plan for us?" That's why it's so important for a husband and wife to communicate about money, because together a better balance can be attained.

One counselee thought his wife was the biggest spendthrift in the world. He was afraid she would spend all their money if she had access to it. So he managed their budget with little or no input from her. It was an area of real friction because she felt she was being treated like a child (which she was). Then God put this man under conviction that he needed to change his attitude. As it says in 1 Peter 3:7, "You husbands in the same way, live with your wives in an understanding way, as with someone weaker, since she is a woman; and show her honor as a fellow heir of the grace of life, so that your prayers will not be hindered." This admonition is pretty stern. If you don't treat your wife as your fellow heir (partner), God will not answer your prayers. So this man's choice was this: "Do I treat my wife as my partner or go through life with muted prayers?" With great fear and trepidation, he turned all the finances over to his wife. He let her write the checks, balance the checkbook, and pay the bills. Do you know what he discovered? His wife was twice as frugal as he ever was and a better bookkeeper too. He opened the greatest area of communication they had ever known and learned that God had put his wife in his life as a helpmate.

# COMMUNICATION

The last problem area I would like to discuss is lack of communication. Money is an area of marriage that can be used to develop good communication. It is a tool God has given you to learn a great deal about each other. For instance, just talking about the kind of home you want to live in helps you to learn a lot about each other.

The kind of house we live in doesn't really matter to me. If it weren't for my wife, we'd most likely be sitting around on egg crates and boxes. In fact, my idea of the ideal house is an all-brick, maintenance-free one-story sitting on green asphalt (no grass). But Judy's ideal home is a two-story rustic on one acre, and I get to spray every blade of grass with weed killer and cover the yard with pine straw.

However, cars are different. I love machines and select the cars we buy with great care. I want the best buy, best mileage, and least maintenance; in contrast, none of that matters to my wife. All she cares about is whether or not it has automatic transmission and air-conditioning. As we have learned how to talk about these things, we also have learned a lot about each other.

We have discovered also that money is an excellent tool for parents to learn a great deal about their kids' basic values long before questionable values become damaging habits. You'll find out what's really important in their lives. Remember what we discussed earlier? The way you handle money is the clearest outside indicator of what's going on in your life spiritually. The same thing is true about your children. We'll discuss money and children more fully later.

Money is a tool for God to measure your obedience to Him. God's discipline is for our good, not our harm. As Proverbs 13:18 says, "Poverty and shame will come to him who neglects discipline, but he who regards reproof will be honored." I read a story that demonstrates this principle. It seems that a kindergarten was located in a little town that developed into such a thriving community that a four-lane high-way was built right next door. When the new road was finished, the traffic increased tremendously. When the teachers let the kids go out to play, some would huddle close to the buildings for fear of the cars; the others were continually having to be warned to stay away from the highway. At last the principal of the kindergarten had a six-foot chain-link fence installed around the play yard. The next day when the children went out for recess, they played right up against the fence. The fence restricted their freedom, but it also provided a safe boundary that allowed them the maximum limits of their playground.

Money should be used the same way. Discipline yourself with regard to money, and you'll find that it does not restrict your freedom. It allows you to expand to the full measure of what God wants you to have.

The minimum discipline in the area of money is called a budget. A budget answers the questions, "Where is my money coming from this month, and where is my money going this month?" That's all a budget can do. Everyone needs a budget—especially young couples. A budget has to be detailed enough that it will help you manage money but not so detailed that it feels oppressive. I'll be discussing budgets extensively in the next four chapters.

# 9    A WORKABLE BUDGET

The term *budget* has earned a bad reputation unjustly. Without fear of contradiction, I can say that people who do not live on a budget are not handling their finances efficiently, especially those who think they don't need one. It's better to live on a budget and know where your money is going every month than to live without one and not know. A good budget does not restrict your freedom. It merely tells you when you have spent what you have agreed you can spend.

## WHO NEEDS A BUDGET?

Most of the women I have ever counseled have said initially, "Oh, I know what a budget is. It's a plan where the husband gets to punish his wife." That is not the purpose of a budget. The purpose of a budget is for a husband and wife to communicate how they're going to spend their money, and then to have a guide to measure whether or not they're spending their money the way they have agreed they would. Many people think they have a budget, but in reality what they have is a detailed spending record. The only control they have over their spending is the balance to make up for overspending. But it is not a budget.

Developing a budget means more than just writing figures down on a piece of paper. It means sitting down and talking about your current situation, where you need to go, and constructively evaluating how you are going to get there. If you have children old enough to understand, they should be included in your budget discussion.

## WHERE ARE WE?

A budget discussion must begin with your current situation. Perhaps you have never sat down and figured out exactly how much money you make and how much you spend every month. Most financial counselors have heard this response from couples who have filled out budget forms for the first time: "I know we don't spend that much money. Where does it all go every month?"

It probably goes into "Miscellaneous." Usually when a couple fills out their budget sheet for the first time, I know that approximately two-thirds of the information will be accurate and one-third totally inaccurate. The first two-thirds of the sheet deals with fixed items, such as the house payment, car payment, and insurance; but the last third, the miscellaneous category, deals with variables such as food, gas, and clothes.

Often couples estimate the miscellaneous category on the budget form to range from $40 to $50 a month. Experience tells me that isn't so. Nearly everyone spends more than $40 to $50 a month on miscellaneous items, especially those not living on a budget.

Once I have added all the figures on the expense side, I compare them with the figures on the income side. Unfortunately, there often seems to be a difference between what the figures say the couple is spending and the amount of money they are borrowing on a month-by-month basis. The difference is usually the result of miscellaneous expenses. Did you ever pay off an automobile or get a raise and, without seeming to increase your spending, find that in three or four months all the money had been absorbed? Where did it go? Into "Miscellaneous."

## JUST A LITTLE MORE

One of the purposes of a budget is to control miscellaneous spending and evaluate where the fixed spending is excessive. There will never be enough money in the budget until spending is under control.

A few years ago I met a surgeon who confirmed this principle for me. He earned over $100,000 a year and had done so for nearly ten years, yet he was always in debt. This doctor's early years were interesting. He had grown up in an orphanage, worked through four years of college in virtual poverty, worked four years in med school in virtual poverty, spent four years in residency training in virtual poverty, and then suddenly had an income of more than $100,000 a year.

He didn't think that anyone could spend that much money. However, anyone can spend any amount of money. It may take more ingenuity after $100,000, but certainly it can be done, and he proved it.

After a conference in his city, I received a telephone call from him. "The next time you are in town, I would really like to have a chance to talk to you. I think I have a problem," he said. "Last month I made $27,000 and spent $32,000." I agreed that he really did have a problem.

A few weeks later as I went through his records, I found he had his office, home, and all other finances linked together. His receptionist, who was also his bookkeeper, paid all the bills. For the month in question, I found that he had spent nearly $8,000 on a Jeep for his son. The son had wrecked his first one without insurance coverage, and the doctor had bought him another one. It went on and on. When I asked him about these expenditures, he said, "But that was an abnormal month. That couldn't happen every month."

But as we looked back over the previous five or six months, it seemed that something equivalent had happened every month. He had so much money in oil wells that he could have bought part of Texas.

He had almost convinced me that he could control his spending without drastic measures until we walked into his backyard and I saw an airplane without wings. I asked him, "Why in the world do you have an airplane in your backyard? Does anyone in your family fly?"

"No, nobody flies. I bought it as a tax shelter because it would be a good depreciating asset." I congratulated him on the selection of that investment because it had really depreciated in his backyard!

As we began developing a budget, I found that he could have lived on a fourth of what he made and maintained the same standard of living, with the exception of buying the new cars, Jeeps, greenhouses, or all the other indulgences he was involved with, including several get-rich-quick programs.

He and his wife settled on a budget of $24,000 a month. Before I left I said to his receptionist, "If he wants to get any more money, call me first."

During the next months, they lived within their budget simply by adjusting spending to the necessary rather than the lavish. After eight or nine months, I received a call from the good doctor, and I could almost see him beaming through the phone. "I've found that we have our spending under control, and three things have happened as a result. First, I'm able to reduce the fees in my practice. Second, we're able to have surplus money and use it for both our family and the Lord's work. Best of all, though, we have peace in our lives for the first time ever."

## WHAT IS A BUDGET?

A budget is actually a yearly plan divided by twelve. It must account for *all* spending, including the nonmonthly items such as clothing, insurance, and maintenance, so that when those things come due, the money is already put aside to pay for them. It's a freeing feeling to know you have the money in savings to pay for the nonmonthly items that normally create such crises if you've laid nothing aside for them.

For instance, let's assume you have a $600 insurance payment due on your car in November. Beginning in December, you must put $50 a month aside so that by the next November, you will have the $600 in the bank, awaiting your insurance bill. If you don't have a budget, that $50 per month (and any other) is usually treated like a windfall profit and spent. Then, come November, it's panic time, and often heated arguments occur.

The fact that you put $50 a month aside for insurance is a discipline, but it does not restrict your freedom. It frees your mind not to worry about that payment. That is the real purpose of a budget. It promotes oneness because a husband and wife can make decisions together. For instance, when you go to buy a car and have worked out a budget so that you know you have $400 a month to spend on a car, including payments, maintenance, gasoline, and insurance, what does that mean? You know you can't buy a new car. It probably means that on a budget of $400 a month, you can't buy any car with a payment of more than $200 a month—and that narrows down your choices.

But this is the point where the practical (a budget) merges with the spiritual (faith). God can provide a car within your budget if you're willing to trust Him. In fact, after praying about it, you may decide that God's best is to keep the car you have and save until you can afford a better one. As you learn to be faithful in a small thing, God will entrust bigger things to you. "He who is faithful in a very little thing is faithful also in much; and he who is unrighteous in a very little thing is unrighteous also in much" (Luke 16:10).

So the purpose of communicating about money in your marriage is to bring you closer together, to teach you more about trusting God, to create a oneness, and to free your minds.

# 10   A WORKABLE PLAN

Some years ago I was counseling a couple I'll call Keith and Laura who were having difficulty controlling their spending. During the first counseling session I said, "I want you to go home and develop a budget together. But," I warned, "don't try to correct three years of bad habits in the next three months. You can't do that. Also, don't create a budget that's so restrictive that it allows nothing for entertainment or recreation."

When they returned about two months later, I asked Keith, "How do you like your budget so far?"

He said, "This is the greatest. I love it. We have our finances under control for the first time ever."

Then I asked Laura, "How do you like your budget so far?"

She replied, "This is absolutely the worst thing that has ever happened in my life."

"Why is that," I asked.

"Do you remember talking to us about controlling our expenses and writing everything down?"

"Sure."

"And you said that we have to learn to control our miscellaneous, right?" (Miscellaneous is the category that eats up all of your money and you can never remember where it went.)

"Sure."

"Well, the thing you didn't realize is that *my* hair is miscellaneous, *my* car is miscellaneous, *my* clothes are miscellaneous." She went through all the things that Keith considered miscellaneous and felt should be eliminated from the budget.

"But," she continued, "one thing that is not miscellaneous is his bass boat. That's a necessity of life. A new deer rifle. That's not miscellaneous; that's a necessity of life. You know," she said, "I think this budget is a little too restrictive. He gives me a dollar a week for soft drinks. But I have to bring back a crushed can to get another dollar."

Well, I also thought that budget was a little too restrictive, so I asked Keith, "Would you mind if I took a look?"

"No," he said. He was quite proud of it.

Normally we use a very simple workbook that helps a family to budget, because I've found that the simplest budget is the best. I have an eight-foot counseling table in my office on which Keith laid out *his* budget. He unfolded it and unfolded it and unfolded it. It lapped over my eight-foot table, both length and width. It certainly was a detailed plan! He had plotted out everything they were going to spend for five years, down to five cents. Every item was budgeted, including one labeled, "Free money for my wife, $5 per week."

"Well, that's really interesting," I observed. "What's the last item down here, miscellaneous cash?"

"Well, that's travel money for me."

I asked, "Well, how much is that?"

"About $75 a week."

"Don't you think there's a disparity there somewhere? She gets $5 per week and you get $75 per week."

"Yes, but I travel and I need expense money."

I said, "Oh, I see. Your company doesn't pay for your travel."

"Oh, sure they do."

"And don't they pay for your lunches?"

"Yes, they pay for my lunches."

"Well, where is this $75 going?" I asked.

"Well, it's going into bowling, and I like to do some fishing."

"My friend," I said, "it doesn't work that way. You've created a unilateral budget. It works well for one person. Do you know how long you're going to keep Laura on that budget? About three months. And then she will suffer what I call the Custer syndrome. Do you know what that means? CHARGE! No one can live on that kind of budget. It's doomed to failure."

Any good budget has to be a plan created by two people for two people, not a plan created by one person for two people. You must pray about it together, commit it to God together, and have peace about it together. And it has to be fair for both. Whatever spending money the husband gets, the wife gets the same amount (and vice versa). If she gets $50 a month for clothes, he gets $50 a month for clothes. If he gets $50 a month for a bass boat, she gets $50 a month for whatever she wants.

It must be a plan that is fair for both husband and wife, because a good marriage is a partnership. If you can learn that in your marriage, you'll have the best communication tool available. If you don't, you'll have the biggest arguments imaginable. This is typically what's happening in America today.

## SUMMARY

What, then, is a budget? It is simply a plan to manage the money in your home. There is nothing magical about a budget, however. It will not work by itself; you must put it into practice.

Every area of your spending must be reviewed to determine if you are spending the correct amount. If you're not, you must decide how you can adjust. A budget, if used properly, should help determine what kind of a home you can afford, what kind of a car you can drive, how much insurance you should have, even what kind of clothes you can wear.

Your budget should be a reflection of you. It should be a plan to bring peace, not conflict, into your home. If, as husband and wife, you find that you cannot agree on a budget by yourselves, consult a pastor or a counselor in Christian financial service. Ask him or her to help you develop a budget and act as a sounding board. "Without consultation, plans are frustrated, but with many counselors they succeed" (Prov. 15:22).

## WHO NEEDS TO BUDGET?

Obviously, those who are in debt need to budget. Why? Because they're spending more than they make. The budget is a plan to balance spending with income.

Others who are not in debt also need a budget. Why? Because it's also a plan for controlling spending. A budget should help determine where to cut back to develop a surplus. It's that surplus that God is able to use to enhance both your lives and His work.

Next I'll help you go through a typical budget, item by item, to determine how much should fit into each category. I would suggest that you read through this entire section before you attempt to develop a budget. After you have finished this next section, refer to appendix B as your guide.

# 11   ESTABLISHING A BUDGET

In this section, we're going to look at how to develop a budget. Remember that a budget is nothing more than a plan for how you're going to handle your money over the next year. As I said earlier, when talking about a budget, it's crucial to remember that it is a plan for managing *all* of your money over the next year. We're going to divide it into monthly segments because most families handle their money on a month-by-month basis.

If I were a pastor, which I am not, I would never marry a couple who had not first developed a budget, showing me how they were going to spend their money over the next year. Once they had done that, I would assign them to an older couple in my church who would then meet with them once a month for the next twelve months to ensure they were living on their budget. After twelve months, they would know how to manage their money properly. By just doing that one simple thing, we would make the vast majority of new marriages secure.

Without a doubt, a budget will restrict your spending. As I said earlier, it's a lot of fun to get into debt. In fact, there's practically nothing more fun than getting into debt. However, getting out of debt is painful. The principle of getting out of debt is simple. Reverse the process by which you got into debt. If you got into debt by overspending, you get out of debt by underspending. Not only do you have to cut back to where you don't borrow anymore, but you also must cut back enough to retire debts, with interest, and that's pretty tough.

Jack and Penny were a young couple who had a ball getting into debt. Jack had accumulated nearly $16,000 in school loans while in college. Penny had financed much of her college also, but primarily through teaching grants—each year she worked as a teacher, a portion of her bill was paid. In about ten years, she would be totally debt-free.

Jack's dad, a pastor, died a year before Jack's graduation, and his mom simply went into a shell for two years. Jack's last year was spent working a full-time job and going to school. His mom gave him her credit cards to use with virtually no guidelines except that he had to pay his own bills.

By graduation, Jack owed nearly $4,000 on credit card bills for purchases including tires, clothes, and food. He knew vaguely what he owed but felt it was "manageable." When he and Penny got married, Jack charged their honeymoon, a stereo, furniture, a TV, even the utilities for their apartment.

Jack's plan had always been to work a couple of years to pay off his debts and then go on to seminary—a noble ambition, but one that turned out to be very unrealistic. About two months into their marriage, Penny began to notice the volume of bills they received each month. Coming from a missionary family, she had never seen how nasty creditors can get, because her parents never borrowed money.

She asked Jack about the bills and late notices. He said it had to be some mistake, because he knew there was no way they could owe all that money. He began to pay minimum amounts on the most urgent bills. But basic budget needs, such as rent, an automobile lease, and utilities left little to pay on the debts.

Reality struck home when, at home one day, Penny had to sign a summons to appear in court for a delinquent bill. She panicked and started a crying spell that lasted a whole day. Fortunately, Jack was shaken enough that he sought immediate counsel from his pastor, who sent them to a volunteer financial counselor.

The bottom line was that they owed $7,000 in credit card bills that required a minimum payment of nearly $250 a month; a car lease of $180 a month; school loans of $70 a month; and $100 a month to repay a loan to a family member. Just the minimum payments on the debts alone took nearly 30 percent of their total monthly income.

Fortunately for this couple, they were offered a chance to move in with Penny's parents. With a newfound humility, Jack discovered the truth found in Proverbs 15:16: "Better is a little with the fear of the LORD than great treasure and turmoil with it." It took nearly all of their surplus income for three years to get the consumer debt paid. It will take them another five years to get rid of Jack's school loans. Jack found it would not be possible for him to go to seminary and pay for his loans. He elected to attend a correspondence seminary while still working.

## AVOID THE EXTREMES

There are two extremes that many couples often adopt in their finances. One is to be too lax and not do any financial planning at all, and the other is to adopt an approach that is too restrictive. That's typical of most young couples today. In fact, I would venture to say that most young couples don't know within $100 a month what it costs them to live and don't know within $50 how much is in their checking accounts. When asked, "How do you think you're going to get by?" they often reply, "Well, we'll just have to trust God."

They think they're operating on faith. In fact, they are operating on presumption, or what I call the "bird-in-the-field" syndrome. Consider Christ's parable recorded in Matthew 6:26: "Look at the birds of the air, that they do not sow, nor reap nor gather into barns, and yet your heavenly Father feeds them. Are you not worth much more than they?" If you tend to operate by this philosophy, think of this perspective: Have you ever seen a bird sitting on a rock waiting for worms to come wandering by? Hardly so; every bird I've ever seen was up earlier than you and me, turning over rocks, looking for worms.

If you find that your expenses exceed your income, you must do one of two things: either cut down on your expenses or increase your income (or some combination thereof). If you can't figure out a way to do it before you're married, let me assure you, it's not going to be easier to do it after you're married. Many couples think they can adjust after marriage, and they end up in debt. Unfortunately, many also end up in divorce court, Christians included—something none of them set out to do.

I have never counseled a single couple who said, "Larry, we just wanted to share with you our five-year goal. Five years ago when we got married, we set out to get so miserably into debt that I can't stand my wife and she can't stand me. We don't ever pray together and we don't ever go to church anymore, but we are right where we wanted to be." No couple wants that. Do you know what they say? "How in the world did this happen? How did we let ourselves get into a mess like this? What can we do to get out of it?" The best thing you can do is never let it happen in the first place.

## A BALANCED BUDGET

Most couples have some gaping holes in their budgets. These holes are budget categories that have been excluded, such as clothing, entertainment, and vacations. That's fine if you're never going to need those things. But most of us do, and to leave them out makes the budget look good, but deceivingly so.

Most initial budgets have no allocation for clothing. When asked about it, most Christian couples respond, "We're going to trust God for our clothes." I usually then inquire, "Does that mean that you're going to do without them if God doesn't provide?" Obviously, that's not exactly what they meant. Is it realistic to believe that a young couple will never buy any clothing? Since you never see a naked couple at church, I hardly think so.

## KEEP IT SIMPLE

The budgeting system that we use is very simple, purposely. When I first began to counsel, I went to several bookstores and bought every budget book available because I needed a plan to help couples get started. Most of the budget books were written by accountants, and only another accountant could understand them. They had thirty pages of information to fill out. If most couples could do that, they probably wouldn't need a budget.

| TOTAL MONTHLY PAY: $1,500 (NET) | | |
|---|---|---|
| **1st $750** | | **15th $750** |
| 1. Tithe | $ 75 | $ 75 |
| 2. Taxes | 0 | 0 |
| 3. Housing | 500 (mortgage payment) | 250 (utilities) |
| 4. Auto | 25 (gas) | 100 (maintenance, etc.) |
| 5. | | |
| ↓ | | |
| 12. | | |

In fact, I believe a budget should be so simple that, if it takes more than an hour each month to maintain it, it's too complicated. So I began to consider: What is the simplest budgeting plan anyone can have? It's the system that many of our grandparents used before there were many banks and checking accounts. They kept their money in jars or envelopes. They had envelopes for the tithe, taxes, housing, food, and automobile. In my family's budget system, it takes twelve envelopes. On the outside of each envelope is noted the amount of money to be spent on that category each month.

For instance, if the total housing budget is $750 per month, including the mortgage payment, utilities (average), phone services, and insurance, each allocation would be shown on the envelope, with the total being $750. If you were paid twice a month, it would be divided proportionately, depending on when the payments were due (see page 78). Since most rent or mortgage payments are due on the first of each month and other payments are not due until later in the month, the amount allocated per paycheck would have to be adjusted accordingly.

## THE ENVELOPE SYSTEM

Many couples I have counseled have used the envelope system, and it does work. I don't recommend it for everybody, but for some couples who are working up to keeping a checkbook balanced, it's the only plan that will work in the interim. There's a secret to making the envelope system work. For instance, if you have an envelope marked "Entertainment and Recreation," and you allocate $75 a month to entertain and recreate, when you go out you take your "Entertainment and Recreation" envelope with you. You pay from the envelope and put the change back in the envelope. What makes the system work? If you look in the "Entertainment and Recreation" envelope and it's empty, you stop entertaining and recreating for that month. And there is no other way any budget will work. Remember, a budget is only to tell you when you have spent what you have agreed that you can spend.

Your budget should allocate the total amount of money you have available each month by dividing 100 percent of it into categories. If your spending comes out to more than 100 percent, you have a problem. Obviously, most families won't use the envelope system exclusively because most of their money is deposited in a checking account.

## USING ACCOUNT SHEETS

Therefore, a checkbook equivalent of the envelope system is what most families need. In this system that I will call the "account sheet" system, a one-page account record is substituted for each envelope.

All the money, except for cash accounts such as lunch money, gas, and entertainment, is deposited in the checking account. On each sheet is written how much can be spent per month (or pay period). For instance, suppose your miscellaneous car allowance is $100 per month, excluding payments, and let's assume, for simplicity's sake, that you get paid twice per month—on the first and fifteenth.

| ACCOUNT __AUTO__ | | ALLOCATION __$100__ | | |
|---|---|---|---|---|
| 1st __$50__ | | | 15th __$50__ | |
| DATE | TRANSACTION | DEPOSIT | WITHDRAWAL | BALANCE |
| 1st | | 50 | | 50 |
| 2nd | GAS | | 20 | 30 |
| 5th | OIL | | 12 | 18 |
| 15th | | 50 | | 68 |

On the first you would reflect a $50 deposit on the car account sheet. Then you write a check for $20 to buy gasoline. On the account sheet, you deduct $20 from $50, leaving $30. Then you buy some oil for $12, leaving $18. On the fifteenth, you're paid again. All of the money (except cash needed) goes into the checking account and is spread across the various account sheets. In our example, the car account sheet would get another $50 deposit, leaving a $68 balance.

The way the budget works is that the amount left on the account sheets tells you how much you have left to spend in any category, just as an envelope would. What makes this system work is a commitment to keep it up to date, which will take about one hour a month, and a commitment to spend according to the account sheets, not your checking account balance.

Nothing keeps you from robbing one account to feed another, but at least it forces you to think about what you're doing, and that's all any budget can do. Most people spend out of their checkbooks. If they have money left in their account, they think it's a windfall profit. But, in reality, it's expenses that haven't come due yet.

## SPENDING DIARIES

It's not uncommon for a couple to have little or no idea of what they actually spend on items such as vacations, gifts, or miscellaneous purchases. There are two methods I have used to determine this. One is to review their spending for the previous year (however, if they primarily used cash, the records probably will not be available).

A second method is to keep diaries (husband and wife) for at least one entire month. Then by combining both diaries, they have a picture of their actual spending. But there is still some spending that won't be reflected. One area that is often overlooked in a budget is vacations. To determine how much is spent usually requires some honest interchange between husband and wife.

## INDIVIDUAL ACCOUNT PAGE

ACCOUNT _____     ALLOCATION _____

| DATE | TRANSACTION | DEPOSIT | WITHDRAWAL | BALANCE | |
|------|-------------|---------|------------|---------|---|
|      |             |         |            |         |   |
|      |             |         |            |         |   |
|      |             |         |            |         |   |
|      |             |         |            |         |   |
|      |             |         |            |         |   |
|      |             |         |            |         |   |
|      |             |         |            |         |   |
|      |             |         |            |         |   |
|      |             |         |            |         |   |
|      |             |         |            |         |   |
|      |             |         |            |         |   |
|      |             |         |            |         |   |
|      |             |         |            |         |   |
|      |             |         |            |         |   |
|      |             |         |            |         |   |
|      |             |         |            |         |   |
|      |             |         |            |         |   |

Taken from Larry Burkett's *The Financial Planning Workbook*, (Moody, 1990). Used by permission.

I can remember sitting down with a couple who were overspending several hundred dollars a year. Normally at the initial counseling session I just ask a husband and wife how much they spend in each area of the budget. We go through each category and write it down. With this couple, we had worked our way down to the entertainment and recreation category. A subcategory under recreation is "Vacation." I asked the husband, "How much do you spend a year on vacations?"

"Oh, about $300."

His wife said, "Now, honey," and after thinking about it, he concluded, "Well, $500." His wife said, "Now, honey." (That's why I always counsel two people. You get much better answers.)

Finally, four "now, honeys" later, we were up to about $1,200. I said, "Okay, $1,200 a year for vacations. That's $100 a month. I want you to save $100 each month for vacations."

"For goodness' sake, I can't afford $100 a month for vacations," he exclaimed.

"Right," I said, "you can't afford $100 a month for vacations." That's where about $800 a year in credit card expenses were coming from. They also overspent about $400 a year at Christmas and $300 more than they could afford on birthdays and anniversaries. The result was $7,000 in credit card debts with no way to pay them.

I would hope that by this time you recognize the need to develop a budget. If you're not married yet, you have a great advantage in that you and your fiancé(e) can plan ahead and avoid most of the financial problems that other couples frequently experience. If you're newly married, now's the time to start. If you're already having financial difficulties, don't wait. Start as soon as possible.

Hopefully you also have a grasp of some important principles of budgeting:

# GIVE GOD'S PART FIRST

"Honor the LORD from your wealth and from the first of all your produce; so your barns will be filled with plenty and your vats will overflow with new wine" (Prov. 3:9–10).

The foundation for any family financial plan must be built upon God's Word. Throughout His Word, giving a portion of one's wealth is described as essential to our receiving God's wisdom. This is not for God's benefit, but for ours. The willingness to surrender to God a portion of what we have is the external evidence of an internal commitment.

There will never be "enough" to give. You must simply commit that portion to God and adjust the rest accordingly. When you do this willingly and obediently, God promises to provide His wisdom to manage the rest. "There is one who scatters, and yet increases all the more, and there is one who withholds what is justly due, and yet it results only in want" (Prov. 11:24).

## DEVELOP GOOD RECORDS

It is impossible to manage your money without keeping good financial records. Here are some ideas on how to keep good records.

1. Use a good double-entry ledger where all checks and bank expenses are posted.

2. Use a ledger-type checkbook (or even better, one with a duplicate copy).

3. Keep a budget book defining the amounts to be spent on each household expense each month. This should be simple but complete.

4. Use a budgeting software or app that allows you to customize your budget and track your expenses.

We will review the specifics of budgeting in more detail a little later.

# DIVIDE THE RESPONSIBILITIES IN THE HOME

It is important for both husband and wife to recognize their joint responsibilities in the home. It is sometimes taught that finances are the husband's sole responsibility. That simply is not true. God put two different people together, neither of whom is superior or inferior.

The husband is the final authority in the home, but God also assigned some responsibility and authority to the wife. If the wife in the home can manage finances better than the husband, she ought to be the bookkeeper. In fact, wives are the bookkeepers in over 80 percent of the homes. And there is nothing wrong with this. We must put aside once and for all this nonsense that somehow the authority in the home is undermined when the wife handles the books.

But this does not mean that when finances are a mess, the husband leaves it to his wife to bail them out. They must both sit down, divide the responsibilities for the home finances, and decide who can best handle what. As far as contacting the creditors and working out a plan to pay, that is obviously the responsibility of the husband.

But deciding how the money should be divided into the various expense categories is a job for both husband and wife. They should create a compatible, cooperative plan, not one based on one individual's whims.

# PROBLEMS TO WATCH FOR
## *BOOKKEEPING ERRORS*

It is impossible to have a home budget without balancing your checkbook. If you cannot balance your records, ask the customer service department at your bank for help. Here are some things you should do to help keep a good checkbook.

1. Use a ledger-type checkbook (as opposed to a stub type).

2. Before you tear out the first check, write in each check number.

3. Before you tear out a check, record the information in the ledger.

4. One spouse should keep the ledger and the checkbook so that only one person is actually making entries.

5. Balance the ledger every month without exception.

## HIDDEN DEBTS

Hidden debts usually include bills that do not come due on a monthly basis. Your budget must provide for these. If it doesn't, such expenses will take all the surplus money for a whole month when they come due.

An example of a hidden debt is insurance that is paid on a yearly basis. The needed amount should be divided by twelve and put aside every month.

Since dental and medical bills don't come due every month, estimate how much you spend on a yearly basis, divide that amount by twelve, and put aside that money every month also.

The same thing is true for clothing, automobile repairs, vacations, and so on. Failure to do this will ultimately wreck your budget. Other debts that are commonly overlooked are magazine subscriptions, credit owed to family or friends, taxes, and investments.

## IMPULSE ITEMS

Impulse items are the things you always wanted but never needed. As mentioned before, credit cards are the primary means of buying on impulse. Therefore, if you stop the credit, you probably stop the impulse.

Impulse purchases can be very small or very large. They range from buying homes and cars to buying lunch. The price of the object is not the important issue; its necessity is. You must consider every purchase in light of your budget.

Here are some hints on how to reduce your impulse buying.

1. Use a delayed purchase plan. (Buy nothing outside of your budget unless you wait thirty days.)
2. Check and record at least three other prices within those thirty days.
3. Allow only one new purchase at a time on your impulse-buying record.
4. Never use credit cards for impulse purchasing.

I never bought large things on impulse, but the small things were still impulse purchases. Tools were my weakness. I would go into a department store and see all kinds of tools that I never needed but always wanted. Since my budget couldn't stand the strain, I decided to break the habit.

I began by posting an impulse buying chart on my bedroom door. I determined not to buy anything that cost $10 or more unless I waited thirty days and got three more prices. Also, I could not have more than one item on my list at a time. I continued that plan for over six months without purchasing a single item on my chart. The reason was obvious: once I left the store, the impulse passed, and before the thirty days were out, I'd identified something else I wanted more. Later I discovered a plan that was infallible: stay out of the stores.

## GIFTS

It is unfortunate that we place so much importance on gifts. But since we do, they should be a part of the budget. You should consider the amount you will spend on gifts every year and plan for their purchase.

Regardless of your financial status, in debt or otherwise, determine to bring gift giving under control. Here are a few hints that may help you.

1. Keep an event calendar during the year and plan ahead for the gifts. Buy on sale. Shop for birthdays and anniversaries ahead of time so you don't have to buy quickly.

2. Initiate some family crafts and make some of the gifts that you need. Not only will making gifts help bring your family together, but they also reflect more love.

3. Draw names for selected gifts rather than giving each family member something.

4. Do not buy gifts on credit. Credit reflects very little love.

5. Help your children earn money for gifts. You also can help your children be aware of others' needs. Perhaps rather than giving a family member a gift, they could give to someone who really needs it.

Next I'll go, item by item, through a typical family budget and give guideline percentages for each category. To help you be better stewards, I also will offer suggestions I have gleaned from counseling many couples.

# 12   THE GUIDELINE BUDGET

## CATEGORY 1: HOUSING

The largest category in most budgets is "Housing." Average-income families struggle most with this category. An "average" couple earns about $55,000 a year, and they are between the ages of twenty-four and twenty-nine and have two children. They're operating off two salaries and have less than two weeks' income in savings. About 60 percent of couples below the age of thirty-five rent, and about 35 percent are buying a home. The other 5 percent live with parents, own a home, or have some unique situation. The initial step into debt for most young couples begins with an overcommitment to housing. All too often they have qualified to buy a home by borrowing the down payment (usually from a relative) and combining two incomes.

I *always* counsel young couples to avoid making long-term commitments based on his-and-her incomes. Inevitably, something will happen to interrupt the wife's income. I recommend that they save the wife's income for single-purchase events, such as a down payment, an automobile, or a vacation, but all monthly expenses should be calculated based on the husband's salary *only*, particularly long-term commitments such as a home mortgage.

To figure a young wife's money into your budget virtually guarantees an eventual disaster. One such "disaster" is pregnancy. Several years ago I had a young wife call at about three o'clock in the morning, announcing, "We have an emergency."

"What kind of emergency?" I asked.

"I'm pregnant."

"Well, just how pregnant are you?"

"Seven months."

"That's not much of an emergency."

She replied, through obvious tears, "It is now, because we don't have the money for the baby."

As many others, this couple had laid no money aside and had purchased a home based on her income and his. Their financial situation was rapidly going from bad to worse. Until they decided to adjust to a one-income home, it couldn't get better.

The housing category should consume about 38 percent of *net spendable income*. Remember that net spendable income means after tithes and taxes. Within that 38 percent is everything associated with housing, including the mortgage, taxes, utilities—even the phone bill. For a couple earning $55,000 a year, that's about $1,700 a month. Clearly, the "average" couple can't afford the average home. Their budget won't handle it.

Many couples ask, "Is it better to rent or to buy?" The answer is to buy—but only if you can stay within your budget. If your budget won't handle the payments, don't buy. It's better to rent and live peacefully than buy and be in financial bondage. As the Bible teaches, "By wisdom a house is built, and by understanding it is established" (Prov. 24:3). Most couples would be advised to buy a small home the first time, put their time and effort into it, and use that as seed money for their next one. By exercising self-discipline and good planning, most couples can own a home debt-free in about twelve years. Instead, the norm today is to buy too large a home initially, trade three to four times when the debts get overwhelming, and still owe for a home after thirty years of marriage.

We use an example in teaching seminars on family finances that I would like to share. Two husbands, whom we'll call Bill Big and Sam Small, are considering buying their first homes. The question is this: Is it better to buy big or small?

Bill Big decides to buy what he can "afford," so he buys a home for $125,000 at 10 percent interest for thirty years, financing $115,000. His payments are $1,000 a month for thirty years, so he pays $360,000 for his $125,000 home.

Sam Small, on the other hand, buys a $70,000 home and finances $60,000 for seven years at 10 percent, so his payments are also $1,000. Sam sells his home for $70,000 after seven years and buys a $125,000 home next to Bill Big, financing $55,000 ($125,000 minus $70,000) for seven additional years at 10 percent. His new payments are $931 per month.

After seven more years, Sam owns his $125,000 home, debt-free, and has paid a total of $160,692 for it, including interest.

|  |  |  |
|---|---|---|
| 7 years at $1,000/month | = | $84,000 |
| 7 years at $913/month | = | $76,692 |
|  |  | $160,692 |

But Sam is not finished. Bill Big has approximately fifteen years to pay on his mortgage. So Sam takes his last monthly payment amount ($913) and puts it into a pension plan at 8 percent annual interest.

When Bill owns his $125,000 home at the end of thirty years, Sam owns his too. But Sam also has $353,521 in his pension plan. The value of Sam Small's strategy is self-evident. As Proverbs 21:5 says, "The plans of the diligent lead surely to advantage, but everyone who is hasty comes surely to poverty."

Once you decide that you are able to afford a home, you'll be faced with multiple other decisions and added costs. Most couples would be well advised to buy a good used home the first time. New homes always cost more than anticipated, especially during construction. They lack curtains, lawn-care tools, and a myriad of other items necessary to make a house a home. With used housing, many of these items can be negotiated in the sale, not the least of which includes shrubbery.

The disadvantages of building a home are well known among contractors, and you would think their children would know better, but Warren didn't. He and Sherri had been married about three years when an unexpected dip in mortgage rates enticed them to buy their first home. Warren's father was a building contractor in another state, and since Warren had worked with him some, he felt he could build more cheaply than he could buy a used home.

He and Sherri planned their home out very well, taking into consideration building costs and what they could afford in mortgage payments. Sherri's parents gave them $10,000, which purchased their building lot. Every detail was worked out, right down to the wallpaper and paint.

Everything went smoothly through the initial phase of pouring the foundation and framing the house in. But as soon as the interior walls began to be raised, Sherri noticed a few changes that should be made. It really wasn't much—a closet widened, a doorway moved, a window relocated. Then the fireplace was changed to a woodstove for better efficiency, and the attic was floored for extra storage. The final tally increased building costs by $9,000.

Needless to say, they were shocked and alarmed. The bank had qualified them at the lower price and would not increase the loan. They ended up selling the house before they ever moved into it, though they actually made about $3,000 after all costs were considered. Warren later commented that when he took their time into account, they probably made about $1.50 an hour and it took at least five years off their lives. "The only positive factor," he said, "was that it showed us we have a really strong marriage. Otherwise, it would not have survived."

## CONSIDER YOUR LOAN

The type of loan you get is also very important. Usually a *variable-rate* loan carries a lower initial interest rate. But it can go up annually, based on prevailing interest rates. Remember that each percent of annual increase on a $50,000 mortgage is about $40 per month. Most variable loans can increase 1½ to 2 percent per year, up to a maximum of 3 to 5 percent. If your budget can't handle the maximum potential increase, don't accept a variable mortgage. Under no circumstances should you accept a variable-rate mortgage that has no maximum interest rate quoted or one that contains a "balloon" payment. A balloon note is one where the last payment is significantly larger than the average monthly payment. This is common where a lender uses a thirty-year amortization (payment schedule) but a fifteen-year loan period. At the end of fifteen years the last payment can be as much as 82 percent of the original loan—quite a shock. It would obviously mean another loan would be required. If you repeated the same error, you could pay thirty years *and still owe 66 percent of the original loan amount.*

A *fixed-rate* mortgage generally starts out at a higher interest rate but cannot be adjusted. Choose the type of loan that suits your needs best for the shortest time period that your budget will allow. A fifteen-year loan requires only about 15 percent additional payment each month and will cut the total payment time in half. The shorter loan period usually has less initial closing costs also. However, even if you select a thirty-year loan, it doesn't mean that you must pay for thirty years. If you had a $125,000 mortgage at 10 percent financed for thirty years, the total interest and principal would be $236,940. If you were able to pay an extra $100 a month on the principal, you would reduce the payment period to seventeen years and the total principal and interest to $159,215. Thus, you would save $77,725 in interest.

Be certain that whatever mortgage you sign allows for pre-payment of principal. Otherwise, your additional payment would prepay only the succeeding months' payments, which include interest as well as principal. Also, it is a good idea to write a separate check for the principal payment and mark it clearly "for payment of principal only."

Don't forget the loan origination costs for a $100,000 mortgage can often run as much as $5,000 with discount points, title insurance, and attorney's fees. Be certain when buying a first home that you ask about all costs prior to closing, or you may find yourself using all your surplus on incidental fees and then living off credit cards for a month.

## CATEGORY 2: AUTOMOBILES

The second largest budget category in most families is "Automobiles." This category should take about 15 percent of your net spendable income, including payments, maintenance, gasoline, tags, and insurance—everything that goes into the car. For the average young couple, that means no new cars, no matter what. It doesn't matter if Mom or Dad provides the down payment. The average-income family cannot afford to make the payments on a new car.

Just as a home is very important to most women, a car is the alter ego of most husbands, especially young men. We have created a social environment where even as early as high school, status among males is determined in great part by the kind of car they drive. It's a small wonder, then, that when men have their own families, the same values carry over. They're going to select a car that reflects where they want to be financially, not necessarily where they are.

The result is an excessive percentage of a young family's income being diverted to buy cars. The only way to avoid this trap is to stick to your budget guidelines and don't commit more than you have.

The best value in an automobile for most families is a good used car. The temptation to buy a new car is often motivated by the cheaper interest rates offered as part of a dealer's sale promotion. But the higher price of the car more than offsets any potential interest reduction.

Many used cars have extended warranties that can be assumed by purchasers, so even the advantages of a new car warranty are lessened.

I believe that, for the miles driven, a good used car less than twenty years old beats the per-mile cost of a new car. The best buys in used cars are usually found by buying directly from the previous owners, as opposed to buying from a dealership. By buying directly from the owner, you can learn the history of the car and usually negotiate the best possible price.

A young pastor and his wife called one evening to ask for advice on what they could do about the two new cars they were leasing at a total cost of $500 a month. On his salary as a pastor of a small church and her salary as a kindergarten teacher, they were sinking further into debt each month.

"Pastor," I said, "how in the world did you ever get talked into renting two new cars?" Turns out he had a church member who was in the automobile business. The pastor desperately needed some reliable transportation for visitations, and this member negotiated the loan of a demonstrator, so he said, for the pastor. The only catch was that the odometer was disconnected while the pastor was using the car. Every six months he would return the one he was driving and get another new car, which seemed like a good deal at the time. In fact, it worked out so well that the friend negotiated a loaner for the pastor's wife too. Everything went great for about the first nine or ten months. Then one day an investigator from the state attorney general's office came to the pastor's office. He asked to see his car and, upon noting that the odometer was disconnected, arrested him.

It seems that the church member had been renting out new cars to his friends, and since the odometers were disconnected when he reclaimed the cars six months later, he still sold them as new vehicles. These were all cash deals, so it was thought no one would be the wiser.

The pastor convinced the investigators that he knew nothing about the illegal practice, but he still was responsible for the depreciation on the cars. Since he couldn't pay what was due, the authorities "suggested" he buy the cars. When he couldn't qualify to buy them, he signed a lease for both cars. The result: $500-a-month payments. The end result was that both cars went up for auction, and the pastor owed the $4,000 difference between the outstanding lease amounts and what the sales brought.

The temptation with many couples who should not buy new cars is to rationalize doing so because of the repair bills on their older cars. So they end up trading in an older car (that costs $75 to $100 a month to maintain) for a new car that requires payments of $200 or more a month. Remember, when you buy something on credit that you cannot afford, you don't avoid the decision; you delay it and ultimately make it worse. Don't get trapped into bondage by frustration over an uncooperative automobile. A lease is just as binding as a purchase agreement and usually a lot more costly. Too often a lease is selected because a couple can't even afford the down payment. The result is more debt and more pressure.

I encourage you to save up to buy a car. However, if you're unable to do that initially, then negotiate for a loan on which the interest is calculated on the unpaid balance (simple interest). That way, if you can pay it off early, you can save significantly on the interest. If you finance a car using "add-on" interest, you will end up paying most of the interest in the early payments and very little of the principal. If you decide later to accelerate the payments, you will save very little interest. The best way to know is to ask before you sign.

Of all the ways to buy a car, I believe using a home equity loan to do so is potentially the very worst. Not that the interest rate is the worst; in fact it will often be one of the lowest initially.

But many home equity loans will be amortized longer than the car will last. So the car wears out and the loan continues. This cycle is repeated several times until the resultant debt is overwhelming and the home is lost. Avoid this trap early by staying away from home equity loans. Just because a home equity loan's interest is deductible is not sufficient justification to risk your home.

The average American couple is going to spend over $180,000 on cars, including interest, during their lifetimes. They will never be debt-free because they don't ever plan to be. Don't let this happen to you. Drive your cars until they're paid off. Then save for the next one.

## CATEGORY 3: FOOD

This area of your budget consists of everything purchased at the grocery store, including food and all household products, such as shampoo and toilet paper. For a family of four, this category should take approximately 12 percent of your net spendable income. This is only about $500 a month for a couple making $50,000 a year. So, as with any other category of your budget, it will require careful planning.

Perhaps the best counsel that can be given in this area is to buy according to a predetermined list. It's called a menu. A quick look around in a grocery store in our country will tell you that there are a lot more items for sale than you can afford to buy. If you just wander up and down the aisles picking and choosing what you *want*, you will certainly overspend and still not get what you *need*. The degree to which you stick to a predetermined list will decide how far your money goes.

I read a study once that dealt with grocery store marketing—specifically what people buy in a grocery store and why. It was well established that women are the primary food shoppers, although many more men are now shopping as two-income families grow. Grocery stores love for men to shop because they buy an average of 10 to 12 percent more and tend to buy more expensive items.

The survey demonstrated that most shoppers have predetermined routes they take through the aisles and that most tend to buy more when the shopping cart is empty. The science of shelf layout was duly noted. Shoppers will be attracted to the items that are within easy reach. So most "junk" food is placed at eye level, if possible. Staple products such as salt, flour, rice, and sugar can be stocked virtually anywhere if they are clearly identified, and most shoppers will find them because they need those items.

Most shoppers take from one to three seconds to select the brands they want, so name recognition is vital to sales. Hence, all the advertising dollars spent are not really wasted, especially on kids' cereals. It's amazing that mothers who wouldn't think about spoon-feeding raw sugar to their children quite effectively do the same thing through many of the foods they buy.

Personally, my family keeps our grocery money in an envelope and buys only on a cash basis. A good shopping list is made by deciding what meals you will have between pay periods, checking the shelves at home to see what you already have, and making a list of what you're missing. The best way to stick to your list is to leave your husband at home. Men are junk-food shoppers and tend to splurge on foods. Also, avoid prepared foods like TV dinners. They're normally 40 to 50 percent more expensive.

One method that many families have found to reduce their food budget and improve the quality of the food they eat is to join a food co-op. This is where several families combine to buy food in greater quantities. A co-op is not for everyone because it requires a periodic time commitment. But for those who are willing to apply their own time, it can be a way to greatly reduce their food bills.

Before moving on to the next category, one side note should be mentioned. If you eat out twice per week, it will not affect your food budget at all. Eating out is a part of your entertainment and recreation category—not food. The 12 percent allocated to the food budget presumes an average family in America eats out at least once per week anyway.

There are many ideas for marketing food stuffs at exorbitant prices that cycle through our economy from time to time. They catch on, then die out, only to be revived again when enough time passes that most of the buyers forget how they lost money earlier. One such scheme is the freezer plan. I'm sure there are some perfectly legitimate home food sales companies, so I don't want to paint everyone with the same brush. But, in general, home food sales (usually called freezer plans) are the most expensive food purchases most families have ever made.

The way most home plans work is that you commit to buy a given amount of your frozen foods from the company each month at a discounted rate. If you don't have a large freezer, you must buy one. The company will sell you one and finance it also. The pressure to buy the freezer is tremendous. It's usually presented as a failure to feed your family adequately if you don't have the freezer plan.

The catch here is that although the foods are good and often reasonably priced, they are foods that most families do not eat regularly.

The average family ends up abandoning the plan in about four or five months and making freezer payments for the next four years.

The best advice I can offer is this: stay with your menu plans and buy what you need, not what a sales company wants you to buy.

## CATEGORY 4: INSURANCE

The average family will spend about 5 percent of their net income on life and disability insurance. This percentage assumes that you are covered by a group health insurance plan that is paid by the employer. If not, this category may consume 10 percent or more of your income. Obviously, if a higher percentage is spent on insurance, then the difference must be taken out of other categories.

One alternative to very expensive health insurance may be a major medical policy. Major medical insurance usually has a high deductible and is designed to cover major illnesses rather than routine problems. Usually, the cost is less than half of what most health insurance plans would be. Another good option is to supplement your major medical policy with a medical savings account, which allows you to set aside tax-exempt funds for medical expenses.

You will find a complete discussion on the subject of insurance in chapter 16. Suffice it to say, when budgeting for insurance with limited funds available, you must make your decision based on a plan that fits your needs, not on a salesperson's suggestions.

## CATEGORY 5: ENTERTAINMENT AND RECREATION

Entertainment and recreation should consume about 5 percent of your spending. That includes eating out, movies, sporting events, health clubs, vacations, and so on. Obviously that is not a lot of money. It means an average-income couple cannot go to Acapulco for their vacation—at least, not unless somebody else is paying for it. For a couple with a $50,000-a-year gross income, this allows about $200 a month for all entertainment and recreation, including vacations. They must be realistic about what they can and cannot spend.

Let's assume you allocate approximately $1,000 a year for vacations—in round numbers, about $80 per month. This money should be left in a special savings account. Otherwise, you'll be tempted to spend it, month by month. Even so, it requires a great deal of self-discipline not to overspend. Vacations are a primary source of credit card debt accumulation. Couples overspend on vacations each year using credit cards to supplement their budgets. Quite often, the previous year's debt is not paid off before vacation time comes again. As the debts pile up, there is a greater tendency to want to "get away from it all."

There are some cost-saving alternatives available. For instance, if you want to go to Disney World, make contact with a church in the Orlando area. See if there is a couple in the area who would like to trade homes with you during your vacation time.

Another idea is to do volunteer work with a church in the area where you would like to vacation. Often the church will provide a week of free housing for a week of volunteer work. There are many ideas if you're willing to look for them. The certainty is, God always has an alternative to debt. Once you have committed yourselves to living within the means God has provided, it opens all kinds of opportunities to experience His blessings in practical ways, like vacations. As Jesus said, "If you then, being evil, know how to give good gifts to your children, how much more will your Father who is in heaven give what is good to those who ask Him!" (Matt. 7:11). I have witnessed this in the lives of many couples over the years as they learned to trust God.

Mike and Jan came in for help with their finances. They had experienced a string of what most of us would call bad luck. In reality, these are often the trials that God allows to come into our lives to teach us where our real source of help is.

For the previous four years, they had been trying to take a vacation trip through the West. Their children were growing up rapidly, and Mike felt that one long trip would allow them to share some lasting memories. But each summer something happened. One year their house caught on fire and required extensive repairs, which drained their finances. The next year Jan's mom became very ill, which necessitated a trip north. The next year it was a car that drove right through their bedroom wall and demolished both their bedroom and their budget because the driver was uninsured. Needless to say, they were both getting very weary and questioning, "What next?"

The last straw came when they had their car loaded to go on vacation. A shorted wire caught fire and destroyed their car—totally. They said they knew it was time to give up and concede that they were never going to make their "dream" trip.

My question was, "Are you going to quit so easily?" It took about five minutes to get them calmed down enough to ask the second question: "Have you ever really surrendered this area over to God and asked Him to help you take the vacation you desire?" They hadn't because, as most Christians seem to believe, they didn't think God was interested in vacations. And yet, God's Word clearly outlines His direction for longer vacations than most of us would ever take—one year off out of seven.

I suggested they pray about it, just to be sure they had peace from the Lord, and then share their desire with their Bible study group, Sunday school class, and others. They did so and a Christian in one of the groups said he had a large recreational vehicle that he rarely used and they were welcome to use it for the three weeks they needed.

It turned out to be the best vacation they had ever taken, and they had virtually no problems. It also started a real fellowship within their class as other Christians realized they could share their frustrations and defeats without fear of ridicule.

Entertainment and recreation can certainly get out of control if you're not careful. We're a fast-food generation that seeks constant diversion from reality. Young couples who have come out of families where they ate out a lot will have to practice self-discipline and limit their spending to their budget guidelines.

The most effective way I have found to control the entertainment budget is with an envelope system. As stated earlier, the principle is simple: keep an envelope marked "Entertainment" with the amount to be deposited in the envelope per pay period. When you go out, take the envelope with you. Pay for the entertainment out of the envelope and put the change back in. The bottom line is, when the envelope is empty, you stop entertaining and recreating until the next payday.

This budget system will not keep you from overspending. You can always rob another envelope or get money out of the ATM. The purpose of any budget system is to tell you when you have spent what you previously decided you should—that's all.

## CATEGORY 6: CLOTHING

About 5 percent of your net spendable income should go into buying the clothes your family needs. All too often, young couples allocate nothing for clothing. But this doesn't mean they don't need clothes. I have yet to counsel a naked couple so, quite obviously, there has to be a portion of the budget allocated to this category.

Usually what happens is that the mandatory categories of the budget (housing, automobile, food, insurance) consume all of the income and nothing is left for clothing. Consequently, nothing is allocated. But that is *not* a solution. It merely delays the inevitable conclusion that the other categories are out of balance. If you can't budget for clothes, your budget won't work. Once you settle on an amount for clothing, it's important to discipline yourself to use it only for clothes. When you look at your budget and you have a surplus one month, it's not a windfall profit. Allow the money to accumulate until it's time to buy clothes.

That's why it is important to spend based on your budget, not your checking account. As we saw earlier, the account sheets must control your spending, not the checkbook.

When you have children who are thirteen or older, allow them to buy some of their own clothing. Give them a clothing budget, and let them select and maintain their own clothes.

Perhaps the best counsel that can be given about clothes is to budget regularly and buy quality. By the way, quality doesn't necessarily mean the flashiest brands or the highest-cost clothes. More often it means selecting the best quality fabric from an established manufacturer.

Once source I rely on regularly is *Consumer Reports* magazine, which you'll find at most local libraries. *Consumer Reports* evaluates all types of products, including clothing, for quality, price, and durability.

Another resource many families have rediscovered in recent years is consignment stores. In well-managed stores, the merchandise is top quality and in excellent shape. These stores are particularly useful when it comes to filling unique clothing needs, such as maternity clothes, wedding apparel, and children's items.

A friend of ours recently located a wedding dress at a consignment store that would have sold retail for over $500. She paid $15 for it, and, after it was dry-cleaned, the gown was as good as new. She reduced the cost of her daughter's wedding by $485.

However, not every good buy is a great buy. Another friend, whose wife often shops consignment stores, told me about the terrific suits she found him. They were just his size, in perfect shape, and a top-quality brand. When she saw them for $7 apiece, she snapped up six of them. But when her husband took them off the hangers, he found they had no backs in them. Later he learned they were display suits used by a local undertaker to show bodies at his funeral home. He kept threatening to wear one to church to show his friends how "frugal" his wife really was. Then one day they all mysteriously disappeared.

As you consider your family's clothing budget, ask yourself these questions: (1) Does it really matter whether you have all of the latest styles? (2) Do your purchases reflect good quality or ego? (3) Do you buy clothes to satisfy family needs or to satisfy whims and indulgences?

# CATEGORY 7: MEDICAL AND DENTAL EXPENSES

Approximately 5 percent of your net spendable income can be allocated to medical and dental expenses. There is a great advantage if you have group health insurance, but many couples do not have this benefit. Those who do not must allocate a greater amount of their budget. In most cases, it will be far in excess of 5 percent.

What this means is you must reduce spending in another area of the budget to compensate. Additional expenses must be anticipated and the funds set aside regularly. Failure to do this will spoil any budget and lead to indebtedness.

One of the best ways to reduce medical expenses is to reduce the number of visits to your doctor. Perhaps the biggest problem in medicine today is that many, if not most, of the people going to doctors could have treated themselves for incidental colds, flu, or other minor illnesses. I'm not suggesting that you should not go to the doctor if you're sick, but I am suggesting that you ought to decide whether your illness is severe enough to require professional medical treatment. Practice preventive medicine. Treat your body properly with the right amount of sleep, exercise, and nutrition, and your body will usually respond with good health.

Treat your teeth wisely and your teeth will also respond with good dental health. Teach your children proper dental care, including the use of dental floss. If you do, you will find your expenses will drop significantly.

An area of real concern for Christian dentists and doctors is the number of Christian patients who don't pay their bills, either on time or ever. It's understandable that a couple can find themselves in a situation where they have medical bills they can't pay on time.

What is not understandable is that they don't contact the doctor and work out a reasonable payment plan.

There are very few doctors or dentists who would refuse treatment to anyone who was making a legitimate attempt to be honest. I have seen couples who, when they were unable to pay in cash, worked out a payment plan that included doing services such as painting, landscaping, and plumbing—whatever they were able to do to repay the fees. I know of no professionals who look down on these people for their desire to work out a debt payment plan. In fact, most of those I know sincerely respect their commitment to honesty and sacrifice.

Just be certain you're not asking the doctor or dentist to support your indulgences. Before you ask them to sacrifice, look for what you can surrender first.

The best source of health comes not from a book or a doctor, but from God. If you are ill and allow Him to remove the worry and anxiety caused by finances, you will find that both your financial life and your medical life will improve.

# CATEGORY 8: MISCELLANEOUS

"Miscellaneous" is the category of the budget that seems to eat up all your money, and you can never remember where it went. About 5 percent of your total spending should be allocated for gifts, ice-cream sundaes, and so on. I recommend that at least once a year a husband and wife both keep a diary for thirty days and write down what they spend miscellaneously. You will probably be shocked at the amount. It is surprising how much money you can put into soft drink and candy machines without realizing it.

Miscellaneous is one of those categories that develops creeping inflation. Have you ever noticed that if you carry $10 with you while shopping, you'll spend it; but if you carry $100, you'll spend that?

I don't know of any alternative method to control miscellaneous spending except to determine what your budget will allow and *stick to it*.

In our miscellaneous budget we include toiletry items (toothpaste, razors, shampoo, makeup), pocket money (equally divided), lunch money, gifts, and all the other items that don't fit easily into any other category.

I can't emphasize too much that this is a category that can grow beyond proportion if you don't watch it carefully. There is no substitute for self-discipline when it comes to controlling miscellaneous spending.

One question commonly asked by Christian families is, "Where do Christian school expenses fit in?" For lack of another category to fit them into, they go into miscellaneous.

Obviously, when a family making $50,000-a-year gross income tries to pay $500 to $700 a month for private school expenses, it won't fit into a 5 percent budget for miscellaneous. This means there must be sacrifices made in other areas to send children to Christian schools. But average-income families can often qualify for significant amounts of financial aid that will help them send their kids to private school without breaking their budget.

It is not the responsibility of creditors to educate our children. I counsel couples not to borrow to maintain this expense. If it is God's will that the children attend a Christian school, He will provide, and not through loans either. As Psalm 37:25 says, "I have been young and now I am old, yet I have not seen the righteous forsaken or his descendants begging bread." I recall a counseling session I had with a woman who had been divorced by her husband. Her lifestyle changed from abundance to meager existence almost overnight. She had come for counseling at the request of her pastor and was trying to adjust from an income of $10,000 a month to about $1,500.

One of the first areas I noticed was an expense for a Christian school of $500 a month. When I asked about it, she was instantly defensive, and understandably so. Her children had suffered greatly by their father leaving and remarrying the day after the divorce was final.

I also knew there was no way a $500 school expense would fit into a $1,500 gross monthly income. Her response to my question was, "I'll do without food rather than take my kids out of Christian school." A noble sentiment, but highly unlikely, I knew. So I offered an alternative suggestion. Why not lay this burden at God's feet and let Him decide if they should stay in the school. If He provided the means within her budget, she would know it was God's plan. "But," I told her, "you can't hedge and say, 'I'll do it if God provides, but I'll also do it if He doesn't.'" She also agreed to approach the school principal and let him know her financial situation.

The principal agreed to work with this woman and was in the process of appealing to the school's loan committee in her behalf when an anonymous donor contributed the funds for her children's tuition and books. The donations continued through their entire high school careers and often included enough to cover even field trips and special projects.

The provision had already been made, but she needed to "believe" God for it. Too often Christians borrow to do what they themselves desire and then expect God to rescue them when the bills arrive. To "believe" requires faith; to charge is presumption.

Another large expense under miscellaneous can be child care. Child care is a disproportionately large portion of a single parent's budget. Quite often, there is no alternative available except to pay the cost and rebudget elsewhere. Until local churches begin to recognize this as a responsibility and a necessity, there is very little that can be done to lighten this burden.

## CATEGORY 9: SAVINGS

This savings is not allocated to any specific needs. About 5 percent of your net spendable income should be put aside for expenses that cannot be anticipated.

There is nothing wrong with having some savings. In fact, it is a requirement for most people. The few exceptions are those people to whom God says, "Do not save, but rely on Me from day to day." As Solomon wrote, "There is precious treasure and oil in the dwelling of the wise, but a foolish man swallows it up" (Prov. 21:20).

It is not unspiritual to save, nor does it represent a lack of faith. I often ask of those who believe savings is wrong, "Which represents better stewardship: to borrow at 18 percent to buy the things that wear out, or to save and then buy them without credit?" It is important that you budget some savings. Otherwise, the use of credit becomes a lifelong necessity and debt a way of life. Your savings will allow you to purchase with cash and to shop for the best buys, irrespective of the store.

Many families fail to save because they think that the amount they legitimately can put aside is too insignificant. No amount is insignificant. Even $5 a month will help. The savings can be any reasonable amount that fits your particular life pattern.

Be aware, however, of the difference between saving and hoarding. A savings plan has a specific purpose for the money being stored; a hoarding plan is money put aside for no particular reason and wouldn't be used even if needed. How much is enough? That's going to vary, family by family. If your income is generated by commission sales and is subject to frequent ups and downs, you will need savings to cover the down periods. For instance, in real estate sales it isn't unusual to go five to six months at a time with little or no income. Without adequate savings, the result is usually indebtedness.

The same could be said, to a lesser degree, about seasonal jobs like construction or farming. The amount of savings should be matched to actual needs. If, however, you work in a stable industry or a secure job, your need for a surplus may be considerably less. Remember also that we're not talking about long-range savings for college or retirement here. We'll look at those areas later.

I also believe that those who are in debt should have a savings category. Why? Because in order to get out of debt, you must avoid *totally* the use of credit. If you don't have any unrestricted savings on hand and something essential breaks down (a washing machine, refrigerator, or hot water heater, for example), it will lead to the use of credit again.

I have worked with many different creditors over the years and found that virtually all of them agreed to a reduced payment, once they were assured that the couple would use no more credit.

## CATEGORY 10: INDEBTEDNESS

Debit payments, other than housing and automobile, for the average family should constitute no more than 5 percent of their net spendable income. Obviously, it would be great if most budgets had zero debts. Unfortunately, the normal amount for most families is nearly 8 percent.

When the amount of debt exceeds 7 percent, it is difficult to balance the budget. Remember that all the percentages must add up to no more than 100 percent. When two or three of these categories are over the recommended percentage, the budget will never balance. It means that some kind of an adjustment must be made.

Debt on consumables such as food, clothing, and gasoline is exceedingly difficult to repay. When they're gone, so is the desire to pay for them. Also, since more consumables are needed, the debts continue to pile up. But what happens if you find yourself in a position where you have committed more of your income to creditors than you can realistically pay? Remember that you can only do what you can do. Don't promise more than that. A creditor would much rather receive $25 a month regularly than a promise of $50 that you cannot maintain.

Once you have developed a budget and know how much money is necessary for you and your family to live on and how much you can pay, contact your creditors. Be honest about your situation, and then arrange some kind of equitable payment plan.

You may have to sacrifice to get current, including eliminating all credit or selling your second car. It may mean repairing that refrigerator or washing machine that you were going to trade. It may also mean surrendering vacation money to your creditors. Do whatever you must to bring your debt burden back under control; determine your priorities and stick to them. Scripture commands, "Do not withhold good from those to whom it is due, when it is in your power to do it. Do not say to your neighbor, 'Go, and come back, and tomorrow I will give it,' when you have it with you" (Prov. 3:27–28).

# THE WORST FINANCIAL DECISIONS I HAVE SEEN

I have made a list of what I call the three worst financial decisions a family can make.

## *HOME EQUITY LOANS*

Number one is home equity loans. The Tax Reform Act of 1986 disallowed income tax deductions for most forms of consumer credit while retaining write-offs for loans against homeowners' equity. Since that time, tens of thousands of homeowners have borrowed billions of dollars against the equity in their homes, a decision that will cost many, if not most, of them their homes in a bad economy.

An equity loan is much like a line of credit. Checks can be written against it to buy cars or boats or to take vacations. There are four primary dangers with home equity loans:

1. People use them to buy indulgences they don't need, unnecessarily placing their homes in jeopardy.

2. Most home equity loans have a sizable origination fee and an annual maintenance fee.

3. Often the interest rate is variable and can increase monthly.

4. The loan is often a demand note that can be called any month.

## AUTOMATIC OVERDRAFTS

Number two on my list of bad financial decisions is the use of automatic overdraft loans for checking accounts. They encourage users not to balance their checking accounts because users know the overdrafts will be covered. Automatic overdrafts also are high-interest loans that are difficult to pay off.

## CAR LEASES

Number three on my list of bad financial decisions is car leases. Many couples who cannot even afford the down payment on a new car turn to leasing as an alternative to buying. As a result, they take on the highest form of car debt.

A lease is just as binding as a loan, and often much more costly. If you can't make the lease payment and the car goes back, it is sold at auction and the lessor sues for any deficiencies. A lease default will ruin your credit rating just as surely as a loan default will. Unfortunately, many couples lease an automobile that carries a large "balloon" payment at the end of the lease (often 30 to 40 percent of the total lease). Since the car is usually worn out before the lease terminates, this balloon is simply refinanced in a subsequent lease and the payments are increased. The result is a lifetime lease at ever-increasing rates.

The best advice I can offer any couple considering any of these borrowing options is found in Proverbs 22:3: "The prudent sees the evil and hides himself, but the naive go on, and are punished for it."

# 13   THE MONEY BAROMETER: ECONOMIC DANGER SIGNS IN MARRIAGE

There are many danger signs that a young couple needs to look for in marriage. Allowing these to build will usually result in greater problems. When I started counseling, I decided to keep a notebook of the problems I observed. I began to see a consistent pattern that many couples had fallen into. Had they just been aware of the signs early in their marriage, they could have dealt with them. Instead they tried to find ways to cope with the stress instead of resolving it. Remember what we talked about earlier? Many times what is visible are the "symptoms," the outside indicators of spiritual problems. In other words, it's the violation of a spiritual principle that generates the symptom that we see.

## AN INDEPENDENT SPIRIT

The number one danger sign in a marriage is a his money/her money attitude. In our society, more than 70 percent of the wives work, and that percentage is increasing steadily. This can create an independent spirit.

Karen was nearly thirty years old when she and Marty met. She had been working since she got out of high school and had advanced to assistant vice president of a large bank. A little less than a year after they met, she and Marty were married. After a short honeymoon, they settled back into their work routines.

Karen didn't realize when they got married that Marty came into the marriage with considerable debt from a previous business failure. He had told her he owed some money to friends and family, but she had no idea it was nearly $50,000. She quickly found out that it took both her salary and his to maintain their budget because so much of Marty's income went to repay debts.

Within a few months she found herself consciously resentful of having to use her money for utilities, food, and car repairs. She felt like she worked two weeks for a paycheck that was gone immediately. One day, in a particularly resentful mood because she couldn't go out to lunch with some of the other women, she told Marty how much she resented it.

Karen couldn't have hurt him more if she had asked him to leave. He was already feeling guilty over his business failure and the fact that he had lost the money his friends and family had entrusted to him.

Marty withdrew from their relationship mentally and emotionally and opened a separate checking account in Karen's name. She apologized for her remarks but nonetheless deposited her checks in her account and used that money to pay for her personal expenses.

After a few months she noticed that Marty had begun to let her pay for her own meals when they ate out, which wasn't very often. The guilt began to eat at her, and she tried to talk to Marty about helping with the general expenses again. He refused to discuss it and simply said he could make it okay.

A few months later the bank where Karen worked was sold to a large chain, and within two weeks she was released. She was totally devastated and found that because of her salary level she was virtually unemployable with any of the other local banks.

In her frustration at home, Karen began to discover that her problem wasn't the job or the money. It was her self-first attitude, and she realized that God had done the one thing for her that would restore her marriage. She became a partner with her husband and recommitted her vows to honor him. She took a job at a much lower salary and merged her assets totally with Marty's. There was very little left over for a clothes binge or eating out with the girls, but Karen and Marty became *one*.

Beware if you begin to feel like saying, "Listen, I work all week long. I need some money for myself. It's not fair that I have to spend all my income paying bills." Remember that it isn't fair, and God never said it would be. A marriage is not a 50/50 relationship, as many people think. It's a 95/5 relationship on both sides. You both must be willing to yield 95 percent of your rights to your spouse. If you're not willing to do that, it won't work.

I have seen a great many marriages where husbands and wives maintained separate checking accounts, took separate vacations, and said they got along fine. I believe that's a rationalization of living a lie. God's Word says that He created a husband and wife to become one. "For this reason a man shall leave his father and his mother, and be joined to his wife; and they shall become one flesh" (Gen. 2:24).

Nobody will ever convince a knowledgeable counselor that "separate but equal" will ever work in a marriage. All it means is that the couple has learned to compromise God's best and live with it. If you find that's true in your marriage, you need to seek counsel immediately, a third party who's objective and trained to help. No viable marriage can survive a his/her relationship for long. They may live in the same house. They may even sleep in the same bed, but they've learned to live separate lives. That is totally contrary to God's plan.

## LACK OF COMMUNICATION

As I said before, a danger sign in any marriage is *poor communication*. I've heard a wife say many times, "It's amazing how much we talked before we got married and how little we talk now." Do you know why? It's because you had an incentive: to win him or her. Now your motivation should be to please God. Take the time to communicate and you'll develop a strong marriage, which will please God. There are many subjects, other than money, with which to develop good communication, obviously. But talking about money is a reflector of communication. A couple needs to sit down together and develop short-range and long-range financial goals, such as (1) What are we going to do about educating our children? (2) What are we going to do about retirement? (3) What would you do if I died suddenly? If you can't talk about those things, that's a sign of poor communication, and you need to deal with it. I recommend that every couple go away somewhere by themselves for one full day to do nothing but plan. As the Lord said, "For which one of you, when he wants to build a tower, does not first sit down and calculate the cost to see if he has enough to complete it?" (Luke 14:28).

## UNEXPLAINED FATIGUE

Fatigue is often a sign that your body is reacting to emotional stress. Obviously there also may be physiological reasons for fatigue, such as infection or illness. But once these possibilities have been eliminated, if the fatigue continues, consider the possibility that it may be a danger sign in your finances.

It's not unusual for a money-pressured woman to suffer from chronic fatigue. Often it comes on so subtly that she can't remember when she began to feel tired; she just can't remember when she last felt good. She wakes up in the morning still feeling tired and, confronted with an irritated husband, faces the day defeated before she begins.

There is always that nagging inner feeling of something being wrong without being able to identify it precisely; that is until the creditors begin to call at 10 a.m. or her husband explodes because all the money's gone.

Rhonda suffered from daily fatigue to the point where it was almost impossible for her to hold a job. When she did work, she was habitually late because she had such a difficult time getting up in the mornings. She and her husband, Phil, began building their first home nearly a year before, and Phil became obsessed about money. He was determined to borrow as little as possible to build the house, and every extra dime went toward materials. He was also doing a lot of the work himself, so every evening and weekend were tied up.

After Rhonda was fired from her job and became progressively less able to work, Phil began to get fanatical about money. Rhonda couldn't even buy herself clothes without Phil ranting about it for days.

Rhonda began to go to various doctors for tests to determine her physical problems, and Phil exploded when the bills started coming. As their relationship deteriorated, Rhonda's health got worse. She was convinced that she had a terminal illness, or at least some exotic disease, but every test came back negative.

Her loss of income delayed the completion of their home, and the bank carrying the construction loan began to pressure them. Rhonda began to decline physically until she reached a state of almost constant fatigue. She would wake up in the mornings as tired as when she went to bed. By afternoon, she felt so groggy that she couldn't concentrate, so she retreated to bed.

Her doctor put her through several tests and a complete physical but could find nothing wrong with her. After a brief consultation, he prescribed some antidepressants and recommended that she seek psychiatric help.

Rhonda, a Christian, was shaken to her inner core. She realized then that she (and Phil) had allowed finances to assume first place in their lives. The urgent things (a house in this case) had replaced the important things. She asked Phil to go for counseling with her, which he reluctantly agreed to do. Their pastor then referred them to our counseling office.

After listening to the entire scenario, my recommendation was to put the house up for sale as is, recover their investment, and then go find a home that was complete and would fit their budget.

Phil objected, obviously. He felt a personal attachment to his project, which had long since grown beyond just being a place to live. My question to Phil is one that each of us should ask ourselves regularly: "What is more important, people or things?" As Proverbs 15:16 says, "Better is a little with the fear of the LORD than great treasure and turmoil with it." The same principle applies to a house and turmoil with it.

Shortly thereafter, Phil put the house up for sale, and in just a few weeks it sold, at a handsome profit. Within a month, Rhonda's symptoms disappeared. They were stress induced as a result of the financial pressures.

An early warning sign of excessive financial pressure is obsession. If your thoughts continually go back to your financial problems when you're doing something that requires considerable concentration, you probably have excessive debts. If you can't take any time off to relax without nervous tension welling up inside—same symptom. These side effects may appear when you take time out to read God's Word or try to pray.

If a wife experiences these symptoms of financial pressure, she may have taking on a responsibility that doesn't belong to her.

Husbands, if you don't want real trouble in your family, assume your proper responsibility and eliminate both the symptoms and the problems in God's way.

Problems brought on by financial pressures may also become evident in the sexual relationship. When two people are under tensions manifested through fatigue, anger, and resentments, it is only natural that their most intimate relationship will suffer as well. Even when a couple still has good communication, financial pressures caused by debts can so occupy the wife's mind that temporary frigidity can result. If the financial pressures can be lifted from the wife, even temporarily, her response to her husband will improve markedly.

If a state of tension and pressure is left in force for a long period of time, however, it can devastate the sexual aspect of the marriage.

## IRRESPONSIBILITY

A nearly infallible sign of family financial problems is the husband's abdication of his position as the family financial leader.

Usually, he will juggle the books for several months while sinking deeper into the financial quagmire. If by chance his wife happens to see the overdrawn checks or the late payments, he tells her, "Don't worry about it. I can handle it." Then, when all hope is past, he will either do her a favor and "let" her keep the books or simply abandon them, knowing that her fear will cause her to pick them up.

Then suddenly he thinks there should be enough money to pay all the bills and entertain as well. If there isn't? Well, obviously she isn't doing her job right.

The truth is that it takes two to get into debt and two to get out. If the wife can keep records better, then she should, but only after the plans are made and implemented to solve the problems.

## THE OSTRICH APPROACH

When a family has previously attempted to solve their financial problems and failed, a great temptation is to ignore them. Those who attempt to do so end up in even greater trouble because creditors will not buy the ostrich method. I recognized this symptom when I answered an urgent phone call one evening.

The young man calling said he had an emergency and then explained that he had let a leased car go back to the leasing company several months earlier. Now the bank that financed the lease had gotten a judgment against him for several thousand dollars. They were also threatening to attach his bank account and his salary.

I asked, "Didn't you get a judgment hearing notice from the court?" He said, "Yes, I think so, several weeks ago, but I knew I couldn't pay the money, so I didn't respond." In reality, by ignoring the notice and failing to appear in court or contact the creditor, he forfeited any right to a hearing or appeal. When I asked why he didn't at least call the bank and try to work out a settlement, he replied, "I meant to, but when I didn't hear anything else, I just put it out of my mind." He put it out of his mind, but a creditor didn't—few ever do.

After several attempts to reach anyone at the bank with the authority to work out a mutually satisfactory settlement, I finally contacted the bank president. When I promised that we would oversee the debt repayment, he agreed to a monthly payment that was within reason.

This man and his wife faithfully stuck to their commitment, and after two years of paying $25 a month on a $3,000 debt, they still owed $2,800 after interested was deducted. But the bank president elected to forgive all the interest and write off half of the original debt, and in six more months they were free of the debt entirely. The lesson that Scripture teaches on this principle is found in Proverbs 15:19: "The way of the lazy is as a hedge of thorns, but the path of the upright is a highway."

## RELIGIOUS ESCAPE

What happens when someone having great problems seeks to escape by falling back on religious clichés, such as "I'm trusting God to provide"? Obviously, each of us is to trust God, but if our bad habits have created the circumstances, God wants those changed first. We are to be participants in God's plan, not observers.

God does provide; everything we have comes from Him. But He also directs us to use our abilities and to be responsible for our actions. When one turns to God for help, more responsibility is expected, not less. "And if you have not been faithful in the use of that which is another's, who will give you that which is your own?" (Luke 16:12).

Dave was experiencing some significant financial problems due to business setbacks. In reality, his problems were not so much due to personal mistakes as they were to changes in the tax laws that affected his particular business. But as the business deteriorated,

Dave continued to maintain his lifestyle and his giving at the previous level. The income from his business dropped to where creditors weren't getting paid on time and some not at all. When he was challenged by a friend who knew his circumstances, he responded that to lessen his giving (which now took half of his income) or his spending (which took more than half) would be a lack of "faith."

His scriptural justification was that God said we must "believe" and whatever we ask for in faith will be ours (see Matt. 21:22).

His friend called and asked if we could meet with Dave. He knew something was wrong with that logic, but he wasn't sure what it was.

When we met with Dave, I shared what I perceived to be the bottom line.

> 1. The business was dropping rapidly (although through no fault of Dave's).
> 2. It didn't appear there would be a near-term turnaround.
> 3. Dave was maintaining his living and giving at the expense of his creditors.
> 4. All the faith Dave talked about would seem to be on the part of the creditors.

I also shared that God will not give us direction that would require a violation of His Word. And according to God's Word, at least three basic principles applied:

> 1. A lender is an authority over a borrower (see Prov. 22:7).
> 2. We are to give honor to our authority (see Rom. 13:1).
> 3. Only the wicked borrow and do not repay (see Ps. 37:21).

Dave disagreed and refused to alter his position. A year later his business failed, and he lost his home and virtually every other asset.

## OVERCOMMITMENT

Of all the problems that cause financial friction, probably none is more disheartening to a wife than a husband overcommitted to his work. Many women have said to me, "How can I compete with my husband's work? He's totally consumed by it." Unfortunately, it's true. Many men, and, more recently, women, are so wrapped up in their work that they have little or no time for their families.

Usually there is a good rationalization for overwork. It may be to secure the family's future, or it may be because "I want my family to have the best." Often the husband will place blame on his wife because, he says, "She just couldn't get along on any less." The truth, most often, is just the opposite. Most wives would be willing to make any sacrifice to have their husbands as companions again.

As a workaholic husband plows his life deeper and deeper into a job or business, he soon receives most of his satisfaction from work. Why? Because when he comes home he is met by a bitter, frustrated woman.

Because of her frustration, often a woman finds herself becoming snappy and irritable. Those attitudes manifest themselves in a variety of ways. Arguments start over trivial matters, such as the husband being late for supper or forgetting an anniversary. In a marriage with balance, these are a source of family jokes, not warfare. A wife may go on periodic spending sprees to punish her husband or get his attention. Some other symptoms of frustration are unpredictable outbursts, threats of divorce, imagined illnesses, alcoholism, or a total dedication to outside interests.

Randy and Julie met when she responded to an ad he placed for an executive secretary. He hired her immediately when he recognized that she was not only a top-notch secretary but a Christian as well. Randy grew up as a pastor's kid and thought himself to be a Christian. He was honest, ethical, and hardworking. Boy, was he *ever* hardworking.

He had built his advertising agency from nothing into a very successful seven-days-a-week, twenty-four-hours-a-day business.

That didn't bother Julie. She was single, intelligent, and a totally dedicated high "S" supporter. Randy was the typical high "D" creative person who had little or no balance when it came to work.

They worked side by side for a year, realized they were in love, and, as lovers will do, got married. They still worked together with no conflicts of any kind until Julie got pregnant. Then Julie couldn't keep up the pace and found herself at home alone many evenings. She also found herself snapping at Randy when he would call to say he would be home at seven and then show up at ten or eleven.

When the baby came, Randy actually took on more work and more hours. Julie assumed he did so because he didn't want to be bothered with her or the child.

In reality, Randy's compulsion to work was a fear of failure. He had grown up wearing church people's hand-me-downs and making excuses for the fact that he had to work when other kids played sports. So his adult life consisted of overworking to accumulate a buffer against poverty. The baby simply represented one more need to work harder. As their marriage relationship deteriorated, Randy began to panic. He was doing what he thought was the best thing to do, but Julie just got more resentful.

Randy asked his pastor to help, and he and Julie began counseling sessions at least once a month. But as the marriage strain began to ease a little, Randy stepped right back into his workaholic mold, and Julie regressed to her nagging wife mold. Their marriage began another decline even during the counseling, and Randy withdrew to his work to escape.

A business associate noticed Randy's change in demeanor and asked what the problem was. This friend then asked Randy a question he had not been asked before: "Randy, have you ever accepted Jesus Christ as your Savior?" Randy explained that he had grown up in a Christian home and was baptized at an early age. "But, Randy," the friend said, "have you ever accepted Christ as *your* Savior?" When Randy said he wasn't really sure, the friend asked, "Would you like to make sure?" Randy accepted Christ that day.

Randy's friend had recognized that Randy's overcommitment to work and worry about security had to be either a lack of spiritual maturity or a lack of salvation. As Psalm 127:2 says, "It is vain for you to rise up early, to retire late, to eat the bread of painful labors; for He gives to His beloved even in his sleep."

Randy's life took a dramatic turn from that point on. He still worked hard, but he made a vow never to work more hours than he and Julie agreed together would leave adequate time for the really important things.

## INDULGENCE

When you feel like you just have to go buy something to make yourself feel better, watch out; that's a danger sign.

It's not unusual for a young husband who is feeling the pressure of debts closing in on him to go out and buy a brand-new car. Why? Because it makes him feel better, at least for the moment. Buying things can be as additive as any drug because of the temporary "high" it creates. Unfortunately, it passes rather quickly for most people, usually when the first payment comes due.

The all-time record for indulgence was probably a doctor I met back in the midseventies. I love machines myself but try to limit my purchases to utilitarian items like chain saws and lawn mowers. I have to confess to buying my wife a chain saw for her birthday several years ago. That's when I found out she wasn't nearly as enamored with small machines as she had led me to believe.

But this doctor bought one of everything I ever wanted to own, including a steam locomotive. No, not a scale model, but a full-sized narrow-gauge steam locomotive, weighing approximately ten tons.

For his wife, that was the last straw. She had gone without new clothes while he filled their basement with lathes, drills, grinders, and old car parts, but this was too much—especially when she learned he was planning to have it transported to their backyard, where he could get it into operational condition.

In my office, she said, "It's bad enough that we don't have any curtains on the back windows. But I'm not going to look out at a train engine all day."

The doctor finally got a museum to take the steam engine off his hands when he agreed to pay for the transportation costs of approximately $8,000. His indulgent habits were not only wreaking havoc on his finances but also steadily driving a wedge between him and his wife. The outside symptom (danger sign) was an indulgent attitude, but the

Bible speaks of the real problem: "Poverty and shame will come to him who neglects discipline, but he who regards reproof will be honored" (Prov. 13:18). Here was a man without control over his impulses.

Your indulgences may not run to steam locomotives. Few people's do. Instead you may indulge in new cars, clothes, motor homes, jewelry, boats, stereos, or any of the myriad of things we can spend money on today. But if you recognize this danger sign in your marriage, stop and get counsel—right away.

## PARENT LOANS

Another danger sign in your marriage is when you frequently require your parents to bail you out of financial messes. Too often in this generation young people are not accountable for their decisions. If you get into trouble through overspending, get yourselves out. Don't let somebody else, especially a parent, bail you out. It's called "biting the bullet." It may mean tearing up your credit cards, cutting back on your spending, staying home, and even selling the new car if you have to.

Many times I've seen a marriage dissolve because the wife came from a fairly affluent family that fed her money indiscriminately. With the best of intentions, her parents usurped her husband's authority and supported an artificial lifestyle.

With rare exception, a man will resent it. Why? Because in his own eyes it lowers his self-esteem. And whether a wife admits it or not, it often lowers her esteem of her husband. It is through the problems, many times, that we mature. At least that's what James told us: "Consider it all joy, my brethren, when you encounter various trials, knowing that the testing of your faith produces endurance" (1:2–3).

Sometimes God will allow problems for the purpose of perfecting your marriage and your faith. Problems give you a common bond that will draw you together.

As I look at our marriage, I think it has been the problems that have strengthened our relationship. Judy and I didn't think so at the time and would gladly have accepted help from our parents, but none was forthcoming, so we stuck it out and made it work.

We were married in the era before easy credit, so we knew we had to get by on what we had. Compared to the problems young couples can get themselves into today, we were blessed to have operated on a pay-as-you-go basis.

I can remember times when we were literally down to our last twenty-five cents. So we would park our old car and I would hitch rides until we got paid again. Our entertainment would be going to the local zoo and spending our last quarter on peanuts for the monkeys. It might sound difficult now, but back then we were just doing what we had to do. Without a doubt, we are both stronger because of it.

Many times God will allow a financial trial just to test your faith and commitment to each other and to allow you to grow strong together. You don't want somebody bailing you out because eventually you may be faced with even greater trials. You need to tell your parents or friends, "Thanks a lot, but no, thanks."

## WORKING WIFE

When a wife feels like she *has* to work and there are no alternatives, that's a danger sign.

With the exception of a disabled spouse, it is seldom that a wife has to work. A wife might want to work and her husband might want her to work. As we discussed earlier, that's okay, provided you keep it in balance. But when a wife has to work, then you're probably living above your means. More money won't help. Her income will be spent and you'll need even more.

I recall an incident that happened to me several years ago. During a counseling session with a couple, I asked the husband, "What's the problem, in your opinion?" His reply was, "We don't make enough money. We only make about $35,000 a year. There is no way we can live on just $35,000 a year."

So I got out my budget sheet that lists the various categories of spending and we went through each category, item by item. Sure enough, they couldn't live on $35,000. So I asked them to read some materials on budgeting and come back in about a week.

In all honesty, I didn't really know what to tell them because most of their spending went toward housing, automobiles, and food, and it looked as if they didn't make enough.

A little later, another couple came in. I asked the husband, "What do you think the problem is?" He replied, "We don't make but $45,000 a year, and I don't see any way we can live on that."

So I got out another budget sheet and we went through every category of spending. As you might guess, there was no way their budget would make it on $45,000.

After lunch, a third couple came in for counsel. I repeated my earlier question, to which the husband responded, "We don't make enough money. We only make $95,000 a year."

Using my trusty budget sheet, I quickly verified that, indeed, they could not live on $95,000.

If I could have taken the $95,000 income from the third couple and given it to either of the first two couples, they would have thought they were wealthy. But I also realized that within a very few years they would have been back in for counseling, unable to live on $95,000.

More money is not the answer; more discipline is. Until couples decide to live on what they already make, more money will not help. As Solomon said, "He who loves money will not be satisfied with money, nor he who loves abundance with its income. This too is vanity" (Eccles. 5:10).

I think of a pastor I met with the village missions ministry. He had never made more than $32,000 a year in his entire life, and that much only in the latter part of his career. He was approaching retirement, and he asked if we could talk about a financial problem.

His "problem"? He had $900,000 in investments and had no idea what to do with it. When I asked how he had accumulated so much, he told me he had invested in small tracts of land in communities where he ministered. The net result was a lot of wealth.

"What was your system?" I asked.

"Simple," he said. "I never bought a new car. I took whatever money I would have used to buy a new car and invested it."

I asked what advice he would give a young couple just starting out. "That's simple enough," he said. "Always spend less than you make, and remember that it's better to earn interest than to pay it."

Once during one of our radio talk shows, I mentioned that anyone making more than $35,000 a year could become a millionaire if he or she desired. Later, a listener wrote to say that he didn't believe it was possible for an average-income person to get wealthy like I said, at least not without taking a lot of risks. So I sent him the following information:

If, at age twenty-five you could invest $167 per month and earn 10 percent on your money, at age sixty-five you would have accumulated $1,056,121.

The principle is very simple. A little bit over a long time becomes a lot.

## NO TITHE

Another danger sign that many couples experience is when they say, "We *can't tithe*; we just don't make enough money." You will never make enough money to tithe. It doesn't get easier the more money you make. In fact, it's easier to tithe $1,000 when you make $10,000 than it is to tithe $10,000 when you make $100,000. Why? Because you adjust to spending more.

Let me make it clear. You don't get closer to God by making a commitment to tithe. A commitment to tithe is a sign of a couple who *has* gotten close to God. Tithing is not a command or a law; it is an outward indicator that you acknowledge God's ownership of everything.

If you don't tithe, that doesn't mean that God is going to strike you dead. Some people give because they believe if they don't give, God will wipe out their businesses or their families. That's nonsense. You were saved by grace, and you remain in God's grace by grace. You don't earn that. Tithing is not a way you bribe God into giving you good things or bribe God into keeping bad things from happening. Tithing is an external expression of an internal spiritual commitment. The lack of tithing indicates a couple who no longer truly has God first. "'Bring the whole tithe into the storehouse, so that there may be food in My house, and test Me now in this,' says the LORD of hosts, 'if I will not open for you the windows of heaven and pour out for you a blessing until it overflows'" (Mal. 3:10).

## INCOME = OUTGO

Another danger sign that you must watch for is when your income barely matches your outgo with no savings. You can't remain there. Remember what we talked about in the budgeting section? Five percent of your net spendable income should be put aside for non-allocated savings—not for specific needs but for expenses you can't anticipate. If your budget is just breaking even and you can't put anything aside, in reality you're not breaking even. You're going under and you just don't know it yet.

The only solution is to cut some of the outgo. Take a look at your budget realistically and say, "Where can we start trimming?" Perhaps a little from entertainment and recreation, a little from miscellaneous, and a little from clothing. In other words, wherever possible. As Proverbs 21:20 says, "There is precious treasure and oil in the dwelling of the wise, but a foolish man swallows it up."

These are some of the danger signs, and you must always *be alert in your marriage to watch for them.* There are many other danger signs, some of which are unrelated to finances. But the nice thing about money is that it is so visible and so measureable.

Just as there is a need to budget, there is a need to do some long-range planning. What are your goals as a couple? Where do you want to be financially ten or twenty years from now? Few couples take the time and effort to do short-range planning (a budget). I trust you are well on your way to doing that. But even fewer do any long-range financial planning. That's why they end up on Social Security at age sixty-five.

# 14  QUESTIONS AND ANSWERS ON FAMILY FINANCES

Before discussing critical family issues, I would like to cover some of the most common questions that couples ask about budgeting. Since God's best is for a husband and wife to operate as a team, it's important to settle early who should do what. It is especially important for engaged couples to discuss their finances openly and honestly. If a deficiency is found in any area, then seek outside counsel.

QUESTION 1: *Who should keep the books?*
Both my fiancé and I like to keep track of the bills and our checking account. Whose responsibility should that be?

ANSWER: Actually, it is the responsibility of both husband and wife. Any budget requires input from both. Once the budget is established, then the better bookkeeper should maintain the records. Sometimes it's the husband; sometimes it's the wife.

I find with most couples I counsel that the wife, given training, is usually the better bookkeeper. Normally she has more time and is a little more diligent. With many couples, the husband starts out keeping the records but makes a mess of them, mostly through neglect. Quite often the wife then inherits them. Her first reaction upon taking over is panic. There may be unpaid bills, collection letters, and too little money. Sometimes the wife just makes a bigger disaster, if she hasn't been trained in how to balance the checkbook. It's impossible to budget if you don't even know how much is in the bank.

I remember a young pastor who had a rather interesting technique for handling his bank deposits. He used three checking accounts. One month he would put money into the first account, the following month into the second, and the third month into the third. He assumed that the bank would have his first checking account balanced by the time the fourth month came around. So he would just accept their balance as being accurate, deposit his paycheck, and start writing more checks.

You can guess what happened. One time the first account didn't get balanced by the bank. There was a large check that didn't clear, so the account showed more money in the bank than he actually had. That month he wrote about a dozen bad checks, and one merchant had him arrested. In some states, if you write an insufficient check of $2 or more, a merchant can issue a warrant. One did, and the police locked up this pastor. A member of his congregation had to come and bail him out, which was very embarrassing, to say the least. His method worked for a while, but it ultimately failed.

Even if a wife maintains the checking account, the budget must be done together. I recommend two things in keeping a checking account. One, have only one bookkeeper. If the wife keeps the checking account, she reviews account activity online, and if you write checks, she keeps the checkbook. If the husband needs a check, he should borrow the checkbook, write the check, and return it that day. It is very difficult to keep your account balanced when more than one person has frequent access to the checkbook. Second, I recommend that you use a checkbook that has a carbon copy system. The most common problem in bookkeeping is writing the wrong amount in the checkbook. With the carbon copy checkbook, you always have an accurate record. When balancing the checkbook, one person should do it. The wife can ask for the husband's help or vice versa. But once you have a workable system, stick with it. As an old cliché says, "Too many cooks will spoil the stew." The same is true with a bank statement.

QUESTION 2: *Does a couple really need a budget?*
Won't a budget just start a lot of arguments?

ANSWER: I've counseled many couples who tried to "wing" it for a while. Unfortunately, many of them got shot down before they learned to fly. These couples didn't plan to get into debt, and most of them didn't overtly waste their money. They didn't go out and buy a Mercedes or take vacations in Hawaii. They got into debt through a lack of control over things like clothes, washing machines, lawn mowers, and drapes for their homes. The problem was usually too much too soon.

It wasn't what they bought so much as when they bought it. Credit doesn't avoid a decision that you can't afford something yet. It allows you to buy it and then discover that you couldn't afford it. A budget requires that all purchases be preplanned and all credit be offset by monthly income. In other words, you can't buy something that you can't afford to pay for. If a budget restricts your freedom, you probably have too much freedom. Every couple needs a budget, newlyweds especially. Never start out a marriage without knowing where your money is coming from and where it's going.

QUESTION 3: *Should we tithe on our net or gross?*
We know we should tithe, but should we tithe on our gross or on
our net income?

ANSWER: I believe you can answer this question best by praying
about it together. Whether you tithe on your net or your gross really
depends on your conviction from God. Remember that giving is
nothing more than an outside expression of an inside spiritual conviction. If you believe that God owns everything, give God the first
part of everything. If you believe that God owns your net, then give
from your net.

The amount of the tithe is not important to God; He owns
everything. The amount is important to us. The tithe, given as a
testimony, reaps a great harvest because it is the seed we plant in
God's garden. God is able to take our tithe and multiply it.

Paul pointed out that we shouldn't force anyone to give grudg-
ingly; it's a willing giver whom God loves (see 2 Cor. 9:7). Give what
you believe God has asked you to give.

QUESTION 4: *What about consumer credit counseling?*
We have had financial difficulties for the first year of our marriage. A
friend recommended that we use the Consumer Credit Counseling
Service. Are you familiar with them?

ANSWER: In general, their counseling service is excellent and has
helped many couples. I have two hesitations about endorsing their
service nationwide. Since each group is independent, each one establishes its own guidelines. Some do not promote tithing while in debt

and, in fact, will not allow it while dealing with a couple's finances. The second negative is that they actually take over the management of the finances while the debts are being repaid. Therefore, the couples don't learn to manage their own finances and will quite often get back into debt.

QUESTION 5: *What about disability insurance?*
Our insurance agent has recommended that I buy disability insurance. I don't know if this is really necessary at age twenty-five. Do you have any directions?

ANSWER: Disability insurance is used to provide the income that is lost when someone is disabled and unable to perform his or her normal work for a year or more. It is relatively expensive insurance, depending on the monthly income guarantee and the duration that it will be paid. In other words, the higher the monthly payment and the longer it must be paid, the higher the cost.

A wage earner who pays into Social Security has some disability insurance. Social Security will pay a disabled worker approximately 60 percent of his or her yearly wage if that person is certified as being disabled. Whether additional disability insurance is necessary is a matter of individual judgment.

Quite often it's a matter of financial priorities. With limited finances for insurance, the priorities are life and health insurance first, then disability. Why? Your probability of dying or major injury is much greater than being disabled. If you do elect to buy disability insurance, I would recommend a plan that will pay for two to three years. Very few people are ever disabled longer than that. And besides, becoming disabled may be God's way to redirect our lives.

QUESTION 6: *Is eating out as cheap as eating in?*
We're a young working couple with no children. Our lifestyles are somewhat hectic because of our schedules, and therefore, we eat out a lot. We both think it's probably as cheap for us to eat out as it is to buy food and prepare it at home.

ANSWER: This is hardly ever true, unless a large percentage of the food you buy is prepared foods—TV dinners and precooked meals.

It is true that preparing meals for just two people is relatively inefficient because so much of the packaging in grocery stores is proportioned for three to four people. However, the solution to that problem is to fix double portions and freeze half for later use.

Doing that will also cut your dinner preparation time by about half. If you can cook and freeze a couple of weeks' worth of meals, you won't feel so much like you're always eating the same things.

One danger with developing the "eating out" habit is that it is difficult to break when you have children later. And even if you can still afford the cost, it's a bad habit nutritionally, as a general rule.

QUESTION 7: *Who should write checks?*
I keep our checkbook balanced, but almost every month I find that my husband has written one or more checks he didn't tell me about. This really discourages me, and then I get sloppy about balancing our account. But I can't stand to think about the account out of balance, so I'll start keeping the checkbook again. Do you have any suggestions?

ANSWER: I would say it sounds like a typical "you keep the books, but leave me alone" attitude on the part of your husband.

There is absolutely no way anyone can maintain good accounting over the home finances without both husband and wife cooperating.

I would first suggest discussing honestly how you feel with your husband. It may be necessary to see a counselor who can interface between you. If, however, after making every possible attempt to work on this problem together, you find your husband still will not cooperate, you need to turn the books over to him.

It may mean that the finances will get in a mess and bills won't get paid. That's always a risk. But until you work together, you will continue to feel the frustration you now feel.

Before turning the books over, you need to be sure you communicate that frustration to your husband *clearly*. You also need to be sure you can handle the chaos that normally follows. You need to be a helpmate (supporter) to your husband, not a buffer.

QUESTION 8: *How do we decide on a car budget?*
My fiancée and I both have fairly new cars that are special to us. When we're married, the joint costs will run about 30 percent of our budget. Any suggestions?

ANSWER: Yes. Sell one of your cars. Your car budget doesn't have to be the exact amount—15 percent—that I indicated in chapter 12. You may be able to go over a few percentage points. But remember, for every percentage over in one category, you must be the same percentage under in the other categories. Why? Because when you add them all up, they must total 100 percent. If you have to spend 30 percent for your cars, it is virtually impossible to trim the difference out of the other categories.

I have heard couples complain that 15 percent for automobiles is inadequate. I'm not trying to control your spending, only to provide a guideline. If you can spend 30 percent on automobiles and still balance your income and outgo, that's fine. But unless you have free housing, I don't believe you can.

QUESTION 9: *What if my fiancé doesn't want to give?*
I like to give money to Christian causes and charities, but my fiancé does not. Could this cause a problem?

ANSWER: This can cause not only a problem but also perhaps a rift in your marriage. The first question you should ask is, "Are we compatible?" Scripture says, "Do not be bound together with unbelievers" (2 Cor. 6:14). This verse addresses unbelievers specifically, but I also believe the context goes beyond just Christian or non-Christian. It is best not to be bound together if you know you're not compatible in other respects.

You may be at different spiritual levels. It certainly is better to find that out before getting married. I would suggest that you delay getting married for a while, at least until you settle this issue of differing spiritual values.

QUESTION 10: *Should we buy a house as soon as we can?*
We want to get a house soon after we are married, but would it be wise to wait for a while before buying, even if we can afford it?

ANSWER: Unless you've come into marriage with a big bankroll, you need to wait. Don't be deceived into thinking that because you can afford the down payment, you can go out and buy a house. Even if you have $10,000 to $15,000 to put down on a $100,000 home, you will still have payments of nearly $900 a month if the interest rate is 10 percent. Before you buy, be certain that the payments fit your budget.

Contrary to a popular belief among young couples, a house is not a "need"—at least not most of the houses we see around us. But I do believe God promises that if we trust Him, He will provide according to His will. If God's plan for you is to have a home, there is a house out there sitting and waiting for you. The way to know it's from God? It will always be within your budget. God will not put you in debt. As Proverbs 24:27 says, "Prepare your work outside and make it ready for yourself in the field; afterwards, then, build your house."

QUESTION 11: *Should we have joint accounts?*
We both work. When we're married, should we have separate or joint checking accounts?

ANSWER: Let me encourage you never to maintain separate anything, including checking accounts. When you develop a his money/her money philosophy, it usually leads to a him-versus-her mentality. There should be no his money/her money in a marriage. The only reason to maintain a separate account is for business purposes; for instance, to manage the accounting for travel expenses associated with a commission sales job.

QUESTION 12: *Should I budget surplus expense money?*
I'm a salesman and have a daily allocation for expenses. Sometimes I use it all, but other times I have a surplus. Should I budget my expense money with our household budget?

ANSWER: I recommend that you totally separate business expenses and reimbursements from your family budget. Those are business expenses, not related to the family.

Many salespeople live on their expense accounts and end up with a financial mess on their hands. They charge on their personal credit cards and bill the employer; the employer pays, they spend it, and then the credit card bills come in. That can generate a lot of debt. Therefore, business and personal expenses need to be handled separately. If you end the year with a surplus in your expense account and the company allows you to keep it, then use that as the Lord leads you both.

QUESTION 13: *Should we wait to have children until we can afford them?*
Raising children seems very expensive. Should we wait before we decide to have children?

ANSWER: First, let me say I'm not a family counselor, but I believe that children, like everything else in your lives, need to be planned, within reason. I'm not going to attempt to tell anyone how many children he or she should have, or when. Obviously, that's between you and God. But you need to think it out very thoroughly and seek His wisdom.

I recommend that young couples do not budget the wife's money into their month-by-month spending. Even if you're not planning to have children immediately, I would recommend that the wife's income be saved and used for onetime purchases such as a down payment on a home, buying a car, or a vacation. That way, even if it is eliminated, you can survive financially without it.

QUESTION 14: *Should my wife work until my salary increases?*
We have qualified for a home based on both our salaries. My wife intends to work until my salary is adequate to meet the monthly payments. Is this acceptable?

ANSWER: I would advise you not to buy a home based on two incomes, ever. When you presume your wife will work until your salary increases to meet your needs, that's a dangerous presumption.

It would be better to rent what you can afford than to take on the pressures of a house payment that determine if and when you can have children. You can easily get trapped into a lifestyle that has no room for children if you're not careful. As Solomon said, "He who loves money will not be satisfied with money, nor he who loves abundance with its income. This too is vanity" (Eccles. 5:10).

QUESTION 15: *How do we qualify for credit?*
How do we ever qualify for credit if we don't ever borrow any money?

ANSWER: The first thing I would recommend is to do without credit as long as you can. The less credit you have, the less credit you are tempted to use. But that's a decision you have to make.

I would encourage you not to use credit for any consumer items such as entertainment, clothes, or appliances. Those things usually wear out long before the debts are paid.

The best, least-expensive way to establish credit is to save first and then borrow against your savings. For instance, suppose you have saved up $500. You can use your savings as collateral for a $500 loan. Usually, the bank will charge you 1 to 2 percent interest above your savings. If you make payments on the loan for a year or so and pay the loan back in a timely fashion, you'll have excellent credit. In fact, you'll be inundated with credit card applications. Then you'll have to exercise discipline to avoid the temptations credit brings with it.

Some couples, despite everything we've discussed, are going to end up in debt with credit cards. The reasons will seem both logical and necessary at the time. The result will be a great deal of grief and strain on their marriages. So let me give you the recipe for being debt-free again. Preheat your oven to 450 degrees, grease a cookie pan, and throw your credit cards in on top of it. That's the recipe for being debt-free (once you pay off your current charges, of course). If you're afraid you'll smoke up your kitchen, cut them up instead.

If you're already in debt and you didn't get there in one year, you probably won't get out in one year. But you can get out. It's a matter of self-discipline and desire.

QUESTION 16: *How can we buy a home without borrowing?*
We're planning to buy our first home, but I don't see any way we can ever buy a home without borrowing. Is it wrong to go into debt for a home?

ANSWER: Borrowing is not a sin, nor is it forbidden scripturally. There is nothing sinful about borrowing to buy a home. Just be sure it's a home you can afford. As I said before, the decision to buy should be based on your budget. If you can buy as cheaply as you can rent, then buy.

Obviously, most young couples today will have to buy with a mortgage because the price of homes is inflated through the use of credit. Without credit, the average $100,000 home would sell for around $15,000 to $20,000.

However, just because you borrow to buy doesn't mean you have to pay on your home for thirty years. Have a goal to own your home as quickly as possible.

QUESTION 17: *Should I pay all the bills?*
My fiancé doesn't know how to handle money. Should I pay all the bills myself after we're married?

ANSWER: Both of you need to learn how to manage your finances, including how to balance a checkbook, pay bills, handle credit, and so on. So you need to work on a budget together. Don't allow any area of your marriage to develop a his/her attitude. Develop an "our" attitude.

It doesn't matter whether it's starting a business, buying invest-ments, or anything else. Do it together. Pray together, study God's Word together, pay the bills together, develop a budget together, invest together, start a business together. The world teaches his/hers. God's Word teaches "ours." "House and wealth are an inheritance from fathers, but a prudent wife is from the LORD" (Prov. 19:14).

QUESTION 18: *Should I keep my inheritance separate?*
I have a sizable inheritance. My father suggests I keep it in my name
in case the marriage doesn't work out for some reason. Should I?

ANSWER: Absolutely not. Prenuptial agreements are the seeds that
grow into bitterness later. God directs a man to provide for his family
(see 1 Tim. 5:8) and a wife to "be subject" (literally, give all esteem)
to her husband (see Eph. 5:22). If the inheritance is from your father
and he doesn't want you to merge it with your future spouse's assets,
you would be better off giving it back or not getting married.

In our generation, we're not very good about keeping vows. A
vow is a promise, and when you get married, that promise says, "I
irrevocably and forevermore commit myself to you." We're a "if it feels
all right, do it" society. So if it doesn't work out, we can always get out
of it. That is not God's way. I would encourage you not to get married
if that is your attitude. You'd be doing your partner a grave disservice.

If you don't believe in your heart that God has created you to be
one with your spouse as long as you both shall live, through good
and bad, through riches or poverty, even through anger and hurt,
stay single. If you think you're not going to get angry at each other
from time to time, you're probably fooling yourselves. There will be
times when you'll get very angry with each other, but if you have
that irrevocable commitment from the Lord inside that says, "This is
forever," you'll stick it out and grow stronger.

When you get married, God says it's a union of two people into
one (see Gen. 2:24). God's Word also says that you must first surrender your life to the Lord Jesus Christ in order to be saved. If either
of you have never done that, make that your first step.

PART TWO

# CRITICAL FAMILY ISSUES

# INTRODUCTION

Before discussing specifics such as insurance, inheritance, and retirement, it's important to repeat that unless a husband and wife are willing to work together, they will never achieve God's best, because God treats them as a unified team.

First and foremost, a husband and wife must commit to spending some time together alone developing their goals.

The topics discussed in this section pertain to long-range planning. In order to do long-range planning, you must first do short-range planning. So work on your budget first, as previously discussed.

I suggest that a husband and wife set aside at least half a day by themselves (without children along) and begin the planning process. Before you begin, you need to pray together and ask God to give you the wisdom His Word promises: "But if any of you lacks wisdom, let him ask of God, who gives to all generously and without reproach, and it will be given to him" (James 1:5).

You won't be able to do all of your long-range planning in one day. The best you can do initially is talk about your goals and get started. Once you have decided how much of your children's education you will pay for and how much they will be responsible for, at least you'll have a starting point. The same is true of selecting the amount and type of life insurance and how much inheritance you want to leave to your children.

# 15  LONG-RANGE GOALS

The first long-range goal of any couple should be freedom from debt. It makes no sense to do long-range financial planning in the areas of retirement, inheritance, and education when you still have debts. Eliminate all debts *first*, and then use the funds you will have available each month to do the other things. Start with the highest interest rate loans you have, usually credit cards or consumer loans. When those are gone, start on the car loans; when those are paid for, start on your home. If you stick to this plan, in three years you can be debt-free, except for your home. And if you stick to the plan diligently, using the money you have been paying on your debts to pay on your home, you can be totally debt-free. With discipline, any couple can be totally debt-free. It's a matter of commitment.

In order to do long-term financial planning, you must develop a surplus of money. Once you're debt-free, continue to live at the same spending level and you'll develop a surplus. Obviously, it's hard for God to multiply your assets if you don't have any. As Proverbs 6:6–8 says, "Go to the ant, O sluggard, observe her ways and be wise, which, having no chief, officer or ruler, prepares her food in the summer and gathers her provision in the harvest." In other words, take the opportunity when you have a surplus to put some aside for later.

For the majority of families, the surplus years are the first fifty or sixty years of their lives, and the lean years start at sixty-five-plus. The funds you consume now cannot be recovered later. For instance, a $10,000 car purchased at age thirty doesn't really cost $10,000. If you save the $10,000 at 8 percent for thirty-five years in a retirement account, it will be worth $147,853. That's what the car really costs you.

At some point, every Christian must decide, "How much is enough?" That includes houses, cars, clothes, vacations, and so on. Otherwise, we simply consume all we make and continually need *more*.

The question is often asked, "Should Christians save for the future or give all surpluses away?" Everything should be balanced in our lives, including giving and saving. Since giving pays eternal dividends and savings pay only interest, when in doubt, lean more toward giving. But God can accomplish both when you're seeking to apply His principles. As the apostle Paul wrote, "And God is able to make all grace abound to you, so that always having all sufficiency in everything, you may have an abundance for every good deed" (2 Cor. 9:8). Since God's Word discusses investing, inheritance, and savings, it is clear that not all surpluses are to be given away. Some are to be retained and multiplied for future needs. That's why long-term plans are so necessary. As you read through the chapters on insurance, inheritance, and retirement, you need to begin formulating your own goals.

# 16  INSURANCE

Two questions are often asked regarding insurance: "Is insurance scriptural?" and "Does owning insurance reflect a lack of faith?" The answers are both yes and no. Insurance is not specifically defined in Scripture; however, the principle of future provision is. Owning insurance does not necessarily reflect a lack of faith (trust) in God, though it can. However, just as damaging are the secondary effects that insurance is having on our society: greed, slothfulness, waste, and fear.

Americans have developed an insurance ethic that often rationalizes cheating where insurance companies are concerned. Many committed Christians are willing to use insurance funds to do things they would never consider doing with their own money. Recently, a Christian physician and I were discussing the issue when he related an all too common event. A Christian patient of his was in need of diagnostic tests. The doctor suggested that she receive the tests as a hospital outpatient because the costs would be substantially less. "Oh no," she said, "my insurance pays only if I'm admitted to a hospital for at least two days, and I want the best." Certainly, this Christian woman would never consider willfully cheating somebody—but didn't she? "And if you have not been faithful in the use of that which is another's, who will give you that which is your own?" (Luke 16:12).

It has been estimated that the cost of hospital and medical care might be reduced by half if Americans could not fall back on their insurance to pay the bills. Satan is very subtle about the traps he lays for us. Rarely will a knowledgeable Christian be tricked into an overt act of sin. So Satan provides a small, almost inconsequential, compromise to God's standard, such as shifting a personal obligation off to an insurance company.

## CURRENT ATTITUDES

Why is it that even committed Christians are tempted to cheat on and then rationalize their dealings with insurance companies? Several factors are involved; one is that insurance companies are seemingly wealthy and impersonal. Inwardly, many people feel that because these companies are wealthy, they must be dishonest and, therefore, are "fair game."

Second, since they don't actually know anyone at the insurance company, it's not like cheating a person.

Lastly, we have developed such a "protectionist" attitude in our society that most Christians expect too much from insurance. They expect the insurance company to "protect" them from any loss.

Some people feel that their insurance payments entitle them to cumulative benefits, so if they have paid in for five years at $200 a year for home insurance, they believe they should have at least $1,000 in benefits coming. Others somehow believe that because insurance pays the bill (and often their company pays the insurance), the benefits are free. The reality that such coverage is not free is beginning to be made very clear as companies cut back on benefits, including paid insurance, to survive financially.

## BIBLICAL PERSPECTIVE

A Christian must believe (and act in accordance) that *all* resources belong to God. Therefore, the resources that are in the control of an insurance company are still God's. As such, we will be held accountable for how they are spent (on us) just as certainly as if the funds came out of our savings account. As God's Word says, "The righteousness of the upright will deliver them, but the treacherous will be caught by their own greed" (Prov. 11:6).

# PROVISION

God's Word teaches provision, not protection. Insurance can be used to provide where a potential loss would be excessive. This is especially true when another's loss must be considered, as in automobile liability coverage. "A prudent man sees evil and hides himself, the naive proceed and pay the penalty" (Prov. 27:12).

This point was brought home to me as I sought to insure our ministry buildings. A group of Christians had provided the funds to purchase our property, which was to be developed into a counseling center. Even minimal insurance coverage turned out to be several thousand dollars a year. After seeking God's will, the answer became very clear. Certainly, if God was able to provide the buildings initially, He could also replace them if necessary. So the insurance money went to buy teaching materials. In deciding this issue, I relied heavily on the counsel of several other Christians whose spiritual insight I trusted. As I prayed about this decision, I kept returning to this psalm: "Call upon Me in the day of trouble; I shall rescue you, and you will honor Me" (50:15). However, God does not want us to be foolish; He wants us to be responsible. Later, as we were able to handle the costs, we did insure the buildings for replacement value. We were able to negotiate a package plan with a high deductible that significantly reduced our premiums and provided a good balance between current costs and future liability.

Too often insurance is used to shift our responsibilities to someone else. Between the government welfare programs and the growth of insurance plans for virtually everything, Christians have been duped into believing they don't need each other. This is again a lie from the deceiver to suit his purpose. But when God decides enough is enough, we will again discover the reality of Psalm 73:25, which says, "Whom have I in heaven but You? And besides You, I desire nothing on earth."

Prior to Christ's return, we will again be molded into a working body, and no amount of insurance will be able to buffer us from needing each other. The community plan described in Acts 4:34 will be our "insurance" plan. This does not mean that the use of insurance is unscriptural, but the misuse of it is.

# NET EFFECT OF AN INSURANCE ETHIC

Unfortunately, one of the bad side effects of relying so heavily on insurance to buffer every little problem is that we also buffer God's guidance. There is no evidence in Scripture that God promises or desires to buffer His people from every difficulty or inconvenience. In fact, conversely, evidence exists that these circumstances are specifically allowed to redirect us or to "test" our faith (see Rom. 5:3; 2 Cor. 8:2; Phil. 4:12; James 1:3). Thus, there is a transfer of trust from God to insurance when insurance is used in excess.

As previously noted, the apparently easy access to insurance company funds promotes an attitude of slothfulness, both financially and spiritually. Financially, because there is less incentive to anticipate and save for problems, and spiritually, because there is less need to pray about future needs (of others as well as our own). Those who have access to employer-paid, low-deductible insurance plans have a tendency to forget that not everyone in their community has the same opportunity. Legitimate needs often go wanting because others lack the resources to afford the high cost of insurance.

# EVALUATING LIFE INSURANCE

The purpose of any life insurance plan is after-death provision for those for whom we are responsible while we're alive. Many Christians have too little insurance, while others have too much. It always baffles me to counsel a Christian who has purchased an enormous amount of life insurance to protect an estate that is probably far too large anyway. "A man who has labored with wisdom, knowledge and skill … gives his legacy to one who has not labored with them. This too is vanity and a great evil" (Eccles. 2:21).

On the other end of the spectrum are those who have the ability to provide for their families if they die unexpectedly but apparently don't think they ever will. Both examples reflect disobedience to God's principles. As Solomon said, "If a man fathers a hundred children and lives many years, however many they be, but his soul is not satisfied with good things and he does not even have a proper burial, then I say, 'Better the miscarriage than he'" (Eccles. 6:3).

There are assets and liabilities associated with any kind of insurance. To make good decisions, you must be able to evaluate your needs versus the costs.

## THE ASSETS OF OWNING INSURANCE

First, you can use insurance to provide for contingent liabilities that otherwise could not be met. For instance, most men need the greatest amount of life insurance when they're young, because they have a wife and children at home who probably would not be able to support themselves without a husband and father. So insurance is used to produce the needed income. It is substitute collateral for the wage earner. The insured is looking ahead, seeing a potential problem, and providing for it.

Second, insurance frees surplus funds. Let's assume that a husband makes $25,000 a year. If he dies, the family will need a $25,000 income. Let's further assume that Social Security will provide $10,000 a year for dependent care. The family is still $15,000 a year short. Where will the funds come from? It would take approximately $150,000 in assets, invested at 10 percent, to provide the $15,000 needed. The funds can be provided in one of two ways. One is by saving $150,000, in which case insurance is not necessary. The other is with life insurance. Even if a family has $150,000 but wants to use it to buy a home, the insurance provides substitute collateral. In other words, it frees $150,000 that could be used currently or could be given away if desired.

## THE LIABILITIES OF OWNING INSURANCE

One liability of insurance is that it costs money. So you must give up current spending in order to provide for the future. If you need $150,000 of insurance, then it will cost money from your current budget. For the sake of example, let's assume that your insurance will cost $25 a month. So you must free $25 a month in earnings to fund it.

The second liability of insurance is that it can divert your dependency from God. Solomon wrote, "Trust in the LORD with all your heart and do not lean on your own understanding. In all your ways acknowledge Him, and He will make your paths straight" (Prov. 3:5–6). We are to trust in the Lord, not insurance. That doesn't mean to forgo all use of insurance, but we are not to use it for protection or profit.

I counseled an airline pilot who was spending $500 a month for disability insurance. If he had lost his pilot's license, he could have lived without working. It was obvious that he wasn't using insurance to provide. He was living in fear and trusting in his insurance.

That leads us to the third liability of insurance: people use it for profit. I think of a man I counseled who parked his car in a downtown parking lot and came back to find it dented up pretty badly. The person at fault didn't leave a note on his car; as a consequence, he ended up with damage on his car that he couldn't fix since he didn't carry comprehensive insurance. A few weeks later, somebody accidentally hit him from behind in almost the same spot. When the damage was appraised, he "forgot" to mention the previous damage. As a result, he got both dents fixed. He assumed the second accident was a blessing from God. It wasn't a blessing from God; it was deceit. He deceived the insurance company and the second driver by failing to tell the whole truth. It's an easy trap that Satan can use. As Proverbs 11:20 says, "The perverse in heart are an abomination to the LORD, but the blameless in their walk are His delight."

## CASH VALUE VERSUS TERM

Life insurance falls into two basic categories: cash value and term.

Cash value insurance is known also as whole life, universal life, endowment, permanent insurance, or any number of other trade names. Its basic feature is that it is usually purchased for an individual's lifetime and accumulates some cash reserves from the paid-in premiums.

Cash value insurance is normally more costly when purchased at a younger age than term is. In a young family with limited funds available, it represents, at best, a questionable purchase. At worst, cash value insurance can be so costly that many families buy inadequate amounts of insurance at a time when their need is the greatest. Then if the wage earner dies, the family is the loser because the needed income benefits are missing.

The normal sales program for cash value is based on three premises:

> 1. It is permanent insurance and will remain in force for the individual's entire lifetime, while term insurance will ultimately cease.
> 2. It builds a cash value that is the equivalent of a savings plan.
> 3. You are actually "buying" the cash value insurance, while you merely "rent" term.

Let's examine each of these statements from the viewpoint of the family.

What does permanent insurance really mean? The insurance is available for the entire lifetime of the insured, but so are the monthly premiums. Some policies can be "paid up" in a given number of years or at a predetermined age, but the costs are higher. Usually these plans, called minimum deposit, involve taking out loans against the policy to make future premiums. These reduce the amount of death benefits available.

It's important to note that in most plans the cash accumulation really belongs to the insurance company. If the insured dies, his family receives only the face value of the policy, not its value plus the cash accumulated. If the cash is borrowed prior to death, interest must be paid to the insurance company. If it is not repaid prior to the death of the insured, the outstanding loan is deducted from the proceeds.

However, if the policy pays dividends, the dividends do revert to the owner or beneficiaries.

So much misinformation has been presented about life insurance that it is difficult to separate fact from fiction. The certainty is that no one plan fits everyone. You must decide to buy what you need at a price you can afford. For most young couples, term insurance fills their need for after-death provision and better fits their budget.

Term insurance means insurance that is sold for a determinable number of years. Most term policies do not accumulate any cash reserves and are therefore insurance only. There are two basic types of term insurance: decreasing term and level term. In decreasing term, the cost (payments) stay constant, but the face value or face benefit decreases as prescribed (annually, five years, ten years, and so on). In level term, the cost increases for the period selected while the face value stays the same. Simply stated:

> Decreasing term = consistent cost and decreasing payout
> Level term = increasing cost and constant payout

Decreasing term can usually be selected for periods of one to twenty years.

Which insurance is best for a young family's needs? I believe level term is better because the need for insurance in a family does not decrease at a predictable rate, as the decreasing term policy does.

For example, assume that a thirty-five-year-old father of two young children bought a $100,000 decreasing term policy. In ten years his policy would be worth approximately $80,000, but his insurance needs would not have declined; in fact, they may well have increased.

With a level term policy, his premiums would have increased but the insurance coverage would have remained the same. Additional coverage could be purchased for the period of higher need.

## COST COMPARISON

Is cash value insurance less expensive since it accumulates a cash reserve?

It is noteworthy that most cash value policies at some point actually accumulate more cash reserves from interest and dividends paid than the yearly premiums. Does this mean the insurance is free? Not really, as this example illustrates.

Assume that a man thirty years old needs $100,000 of insurance to provide for his wife and three children in the event of his death. His choices have boiled down to a cash value policy or a yearly renewable term policy. The cash value policy costs $1,200 a year.

At age sixty-five, it will have $100,000 in cash value. If he dies any time before age sixty-five, his family will receive the $100,000 face value. Assume also that he can afford the premium. If he could not, the decision would be one of budget.

The term policy costs $200 per year initially. Each year the premium costs will increase. This particular term is guaranteed renewable regardless of his health, until age one hundred.

The difference in premium cost between the cash value policy and the term policy will be invested in US savings bonds each year so that the equivalent of the cash value policy is being saved. At the age of sixty-five, the cash reserves are as follows:

Cash value in insurance  = $100,000

Cash in savings bonds    = $127,000

It is also important to remember that if the husband dies before age sixty-five, his family would receive $100,000 from the cash value policy but would receive $100,000 from the term policy *plus* whatever has been accumulated by the savings bonds up to that point.

## CONCLUSIONS

Probably the best way to summarize life insurance by cost and type is to look at how much money is available to purchase what you need.

Most young families can afford only term life insurance. Term insurance is much less expensive than cash value insurance at the younger age when the need is high but the income is limited. The older the person is when selecting insurance, the more costly the term policy. But so is a cash value policy when purchased at an older age. You can get the best value by purchasing term and saving the difference. However, the practical truth is that most people don't save the difference; they spend it. When they get to be fifty or older, their term insurance can get to be prohibitively expensive.

My direction for the couples I counsel is this: buy term because you cannot afford cash value. But, if by the age of forty you have not been disciplined enough to save the difference that the cash value would have cost, then convert to a cash value plan.

## HOW MUCH LIFE INSURANCE?

"How much is enough?" is a difficult question to answer precisely. There are many variables within each family that must be considered:

the age of the children, the wife's income capability, existing debts, current lifestyle and income, and any other sources of after-death income besides life insurance. One family may wish to supply enough insurance to live off interest income alone, while another may wish to provide for a specific number of years. These decisions are important and should be made mutually by husband and wife.

One method to help you evaluate how much insurance you need is based on present income and spending. Once you have begun to budget and have peace that it is God's plan for your family, the same income would probably be necessary in the event of the wage earner's death.

Using the following guide, we will assume that a man dies, leaving a wife and two young children. His annual income had been $24,000. He had no large investment plan and only a small savings plan.

| | | |
|---|---:|---:|
| Husband's income per year | | $24,000 |
| Less: | | |
| Insurance (not necessary) | $250 | |
| His living costs | $3,000 | |
| Social Security income | $8,000 | |
| Deduct after-death income | | |
| from total deductions | | $11,250 |
| Income needed for family | | $12,750 |

Multiply $12,750 x 10 = $127,500 of insurance needed (multiplying the amount needed to earn $12,750 yearly at 10 percent interest). Thus, the approximate amount of insurance necessary to earn $12,750 in interest income is $127,500. Appendix C provides a simple form for calculating the amount of insurance your family needs.

If additional funds are needed for education or other special circumstances, these also should be considered. Strive for balance. Trying to overprotect a Christian family can remove them from God's plan for their lives. The same God who provides for us promises to provide for our families as well. He wants us to use our sound minds to provide but not to try to protect against everything (see 1 Tim. 5:8).

## SHOULD STAY-AT-HOME WIVES HAVE LIFE INSURANCE?

Several sales methods are used to sell insurance for wives. The most common question is this: How much would it cost to replace the work a wife provides in the home? This is usually meant to imply a maid and other services. The reasoning is valid only when a family has small children and no close relatives or friends who could or would assist in the housekeeping, cooking, and so forth.

Another reason given for the wife to have insurance is the cost of her burial. This is a legitimate purpose to carry some insurance on a wife. Unless a family has enough money in savings to cover the funeral costs, such an expense could place them in financial bondage.

My wife and I assessed this possibility in our planning and began to search for a reasonable alternative. It didn't seem to me to be good stewardship to pay out money month after month for a contingency such as my wife's possible funeral expenses.

We found an alternative through the Memorial Society of Georgia. This is a nonprofit organization created to reduce the cost of funerals.

For a small initial fee, we are guaranteed an extremely low-cost funeral for any immediate family member. The actual cost would be far less than a normal arrangement and within what I could afford. This same plan covers all arrangements in the event of my death and removes the burden from my wife. Memorial societies exist throughout most parts of the United States.

The principle is this: if insurance dollars are limited, spend them where they are needed most—on the wage earner!

## CHOOSE YOUR AGENT WISELY

One of your best assets is a good independent insurance agent to help you with these decisions. Shop around—a lot! Look for an agent who has your interests at heart and not his or her own. The proof should be in black and white. Ask the agent to thoroughly define the insurance plan in writing, and then have several other agents, including those who sell both term and cash value, give you comparative prices. Remember: "Where there is no guidance the people fall, but in abundance of counselors there is victory" (Prov. 11:14).

## DISABILITY INSURANCE

As with most kinds of insurance, it is almost impossible to describe the different types of disability insurance. An agent can virtually design a policy on the spot if you can afford it.

Balance is again most important. You must ask yourself whether your attitude is motivated by fear of the unknown or by God's plan for your family. A high-pressure salesperson can generate an attitude of fear by describing "horror stories" that happen to other families. But you must develop your own plans, which may or may not include disability insurance. In no case should disability insurance be looked upon as a means to supply all future income. The cost would be so high that it would rob current family needs and, even worse, take away the incentive to readjust to a new life.

# 17   INHERITANCE

Inheritance is one of those subjects that most of us don't like to talk about. It's amazing to me how superstitious Christians are. We think that, somehow, talking about death might make it happen. This I'll guarantee you: talking about death won't make it come a minute sooner, and not talking about it won't delay it one minute longer. That's up to God.

About 80 percent of all Americans die without valid wills. In others words, they haven't left the basic details telling how they want to distribute their assets. When you die without a will, it means that you die under the laws of intestacy in your state. The state will determine what happens to your assets according to a predetermined plan. Go to any public library and look at a copy of the state's will. It should stimulate you to action when you read it. The widow becomes a child in the eyes of the state. She gets a child's portion, and the children get individual portions of the estate. She can be required to prove how and where the children's money is used, file reports, and pay for audits.

I have talked to people who said, "We don't need wills because we don't own anything." In 1976, three men I knew died in accidents. Two died in a plane crash and the third in a car accident. Of the three men, only one had a will. None had any major assets. Their estates consisted primarily of life insurance that was assigned to their widows, so they felt they didn't really need wills. The settlement from the plane crash was over a million dollars, and the settlement from the automobile accident was about $700,000. These husbands had enormous estates and didn't know it.

For the two men without wills, it took nearly four years and cost over $300,000 to clear and distribute the estates. For the husband with the will, it took sixty days and cost about $6,000.

Both the husband *and* the wife need wills. One reason the wife needs a will is because if her husband dies in a common accident, the assets of the estate can pass to her. If she has no will, then when she dies, she dies intestate and the court handles the estate.

By the way, about 85 percent of all attorneys in America die without valid wills. That's the old shoemaker's principle, remember? The shoemaker is the only man in town whose kids don't have shoes. The attorney makes wills for everybody else but neglects to make his own.

Solomon said, "If a man fathers a hundred children and lives many years, however many they be, but his soul is not satisfied with good things and he does not even have a proper burial, then I say, 'Better the miscarriage than he'" (Eccles. 6:3).

This principle means that God expects us to be responsible. The minimum stewardship for any Christian in the area of inheritance is to have a valid will. As we just discussed, life insurance can provide the needed funds; a will determines how they are to be distributed.

What are the basic biblical guidelines for inheritance? First, God's Word teaches that we should do our giving while we're still alive. The only exception is when we die prematurely. Our basic inheritance plan should be to pass along the inheritance to our children while we're alive so we can see how they use it.

A friend, who has now gone to be with the Lord, told me, "Do your giving while you're living; then you're knowing where it's going." That's a good cliché for all of us to remember.

Too often in our generation, parents are so deeply in debt that they have nothing to leave their children. I saw a bumper sticker not long ago that I thought characterized our society. It read, "I'm headed to Florida to spend my kids' inheritance."

## WHEN TO GIVE AN INHERITANCE

I don't suggest giving children their inheritance when they're six years old or even eighteen. But at some point, begin to distribute the assets you want them to have. If you die prematurely, your will or trust should specify when distributions should be made to your children. I would suggest staggering payments over several years; for example, at ages twenty-five, thirty, thirty-five, and so on. That way the children are older and hopefully wiser.

A common problem is a widow who is left to manage assets that have to last her for the rest of her life and who has little or no knowledge of what to do. I believe that every husband, at least once a year, needs to sit down and write his wife a letter, detailing what she should do in the event of his death. List all the assets, including insurance and investments, and give her counsel on what you would do if you were there and had the funds available. Wives need to be *sure* this is done.

I have counseled enough widows to know that too often they don't even know where the insurance policies are. They have no idea of whether it's better to take the insurance in cash or an annuity. These questions can be simplified greatly by investing the few minutes it takes once a year to discuss these key matters.

Obviously, a wife needs to understand how to manage the finances of the home. I have met women who said, "I just don't want to do it. My husband keeps the books and pays the bills." Every wife needs to manage the books in the home for some period of time—at least enough to know how.

Statistics tell us that the vast majority of the time, the husband predeceases his wife, and the average age at which a woman is widowed is fifty-two. I told that at a conference not long ago, and a man responded, "If I divorce my wife when she's fifty-one, I'm bound to live longer, right?" No, it doesn't work that way.

## TRUSTS

A trust is merely a detailed plan that tells the government how to distribute your assets after your death. Since it is a legal entity, much as a corporation is, a trust that is activated before you die does not need to be probated (proved). So it avoids the delay and costs of probate.

There are two basic kinds of trusts. One is called *inter vivos*, or a living trust. The second is called a *testamentary* trust. A living trust means exactly that. It is established while you're alive. A testamentary trust means it is activated upon death.

There are two common types of living trusts. The first is a *revocable* trust, and the other is an *irrevocable* trust. Revocable means that the donor can change or cancel the trust while he or she is alive. Irrevocable means that the donor gives up all rights to the assets assigned to the trust. For instance, assume that I set up an irrevocable living trust and put assets in it, such as my home, my insurance, stocks, and bonds. I am bound by the terms of the trust while I am alive. Upon my death, the assets of the trust will be managed or distributed as I determined.

However, in a revocable living trust, I have the right to withdraw the assets at any time prior to my death. The trust becomes irrevocable upon my death.

Neither trust will have to go through the probate court. However, the assets in the revocable trust can be taxed because they are part of my estate. If I reserve the right to control them, the law considers that they belong to me.

The most common type of trust for most families is a part of their wills. Let's assume that in my will I state, "Upon my death, take my insurance and put it into a trust so that the assets are managed to provide for my wife as long as she's alive. Upon her death, liquidate this trust and distribute the proceeds to my children equally." This becomes a testamentary trust. All of my assets would go through the probate court, but then the trusts would take effect. The reason for a testamentary trust is to direct the use of the assets and avoid unnecessary estate taxes in the event of a common accident. In this case, the assets would not be totally taxable in my wife's estate.

## WHAT IF YOU MOVE?

Your will may not be valid from state to state. Let's assume that you live in a state that requires two witnesses on a will and you move to a state that requires three witnesses on a will. You have an invalid will. You need to be sure that the laws of the state where the will was drawn are compatible with the laws of the state where you presently live.

## HOLOGRAPHIC WILLS

Can you draft your own will? Most states provide an alternative for residents to draft their own wills. However, you need to be very cautious because many self-made (holographic) wills are not provable in court. Many judges of the probate court are very critical of wills not drawn by professional attorneys. So before you try to draft your own will or buy a "will kit," you need to check it out with a good attorney in your state.

By the way, I recommend that the original copies of all important documents, such as wills, insurance policies, and the like, be stored together in a safe and findable place. A safe-deposit box at your local bank protects these papers against theft and destruction.

# 18   RETIREMENT

Does the Bible speak about retirement? Yes, it does. In fact, the Bible speaks on finances approximately 1,800 times. Out of those 1,800 scriptures that deal with finances, only one references the subject of retirement. It's found in Numbers 8:25: "But at the age of fifty years they shall retire from service in the work and not work any more." The "they" refers to the temple priests. We don't know what the temple priests did after age fifty, but they could no longer be temple priests. Since that is the only reference on retirement in the entire Bible, I believe the concept we have about retirement today is somewhat out of balance.

As we get older we will normally change our work patterns. A fifty-year-old man rarely does the same things at fifty that he did at twenty-five. Most who live to be seventy-five won't do the same things they're doing at fifty. But most can be doing something productive for the Lord if they plan properly.

I recall a study done by a major university. The researchers surveyed two hundred sixty-five-year-old men who were graduates of their school, eliminating those with bad health, heart trouble, and so on. They maintained contact with these men from ages sixty-five to seventy-five. One half of the study group retired at sixty-five and the other continued their careers. At age seventy-five, of the group that had retired, six out of seven had died. Of the group that did not retire, six out of seven were still alive.

The conclusion of this study was that if a man stops working at age sixty-five, his probability of dying increases by approximately 500 to 600 percent. So if you want to live longer, stay active.

Let's look at retirement from a practical perspective. If you're not going to be able to do the same things at sixty-five that you were able to do at twenty-five, you need to be preparing for that contingency. If these are the harvest years of your life, then you should put something aside for the winter years. Or if you desire to do volunteer work with a ministry after retirement, you'll need to have some surplus funds set aside, and there's nothing wrong with that.

But the point is, if a Christian orients his or her life toward retirement, something is out of balance. I think of what David wrote: "I have been young and now I am old, yet I have not seen the righteous forsaken or his descendants begging bread" (Ps. 37:25). We need to remember that.

# GUIDELINES FOR RETIREMENT

First, *God intends that we be productive.* So plan something later in life that you can do to earn a living. If you're a schoolteacher and you don't think you can continue teaching school beyond age sixty-five, take up plumbing. If you're a plumber and you don't think you can plumb beyond age sixty-five, take up teaching school. It's amazing to me that plumbers retire and want to teach school, and teachers retire and want to go into plumbing. But it's important that you find a way to keep productive.

Second, *we must be prudent.* As Proverbs 27:12 says, "A prudent man sees evil and hides himself, the naive proceed and pay the penalty." Obviously, you are going to get older. The alternative to getting older is not a good one. Plan for it and lay aside some money for the future. If you're living on such a small income that you cannot put any money aside for the future, God can still provide for you.

Third, *we should not rely totally on Social Security.* When Social Security started making regular payments in 1940, there were forty-two contributors for every person drawing from it. By 2012, that number had dropped to 2.8 people contributing for every person drawing from the system, according to an article in *Time* magazine. Obviously, we cannot plan our entire retirement around Social Security; it should be a supplement only. There is no way the system can continue without some changes. A simple solution that would make Social Security solvent again would be to raise the minimum retirement age to about ninety-five!

Since you cannot rely on Social Security, what other retirement plans should you consider? If you qualify for an IRA (individual retirement account), consider saving some money each year to the extent that your budget will allow you to contribute. For a discussion of retirement investing, see part 4, "Ten Keys to Successful Investing."

What about company retirement plans? You need to evaluate your company retirement plan to see if it meets your needs. But let me caution you: many large companies borrow money from the employees' retirement plans. If the company fails, and many companies do, they can bankrupt the retirement plan at the same time. If I were with a large company, I would check to see how much it has borrowed from the plan.

What can you do if you find the company is heavily in debt to the retirement plan? Write the company leaders and tell them of your concern. And I probably wouldn't do all of my retirement planning around that plan.

One last thing about retirement: I believe the best potential retirement plan for anybody is the ability to earn a living after sixty-five or seventy years old. I would encourage you to begin looking for an alternative vocation after you retire. I'd recommend going to a good vocational school and studying a trade in your spare time. Pick one that you would like to do, perhaps in the field of electricity, plumbing, air-conditioning, or refrigeration. We're a service-oriented society, and as long as you can provide a service, you can always earn a living. It's simply a matter of finding one that you like to do and are good at. Just hire somebody to come change the washers in your faucets, and you'll discover how difficult and expensive it is.

# PART THREE

# CHILDREN'S FINANCES

# INTRODUCTION

Not long ago someone called to ask a question about a comment I had made on a seminar tape. I was about to explain it when she said, "Wait just a minute. Would you mind explaining that to my daughter? She's been listening to your tapes and it's her question." The daughter was eight years old. She asked a question about borrowing and whether or not it was scriptural.

I was astounded. I had forgotten that many times young children can understand a great deal more than we give them credit for. Usually their attitudes are formed at an early age. They're formed either in the image of God or in the image of the world. Christian parents have a responsibility to help form their children into the image of God.

Remember what God told Eli? He said that Eli's sons had done evil in the sight of the Lord and that He was going to punish them for it. In fact, He took their lives. And God told Eli that he must also die—not for their sins but because he did not train them in the ways of the Lord. Eli was not responsible for his sons' decisions, but he was responsible for their training (see 1 Sam. 2:27–34).

A simple biblical principle will greatly help our children: "In the face of the truth, a lie will always be evident." Therefore, what you need to do as a parent is expose your children to the truth of God's Word, and it will reveal the lies they're going to hear about finances.

It's interesting how banks train tellers to recognize counterfeit bills. They don't keep a supply of counterfeit bills to show them. Instead they give them a stack of brand-new twenty-dollar bills and let them thumb through them. Once they have done that long enough, they'll recognize a counterfeit when it crosses their hands, just by the feel. Once they know the real thing, the phonies will be evident.

I would like to share some simple principles of teaching children about finances that have been helpful to us and many other families. We have four children—three boys and a girl—and it has always fascinated me that we have four exact opposites. What works with one certainly doesn't work with all.

I suppose I have counseled hundreds of couples with children, at one time or another. Most of them wanted me to teach their children the biblical principles of handling money, because the kids were having problems. The thing I remind them is that it is not my responsibility to teach their children; nor is it the church's responsibility or even the school's. God laid that responsibility squarely on the parents, and they can't avoid it.

The way to train your children is actually very simple. It's a principle given in Proverbs that would translate, "As God is to the parents, so the parents should be to their children." In other words, whatever principles God establishes for the parents, the parents should pass along to their children. That seems easy enough. The difficulty comes in deciding which principles to teach at what age and how to get your children to understand. Hopefully, this discussion will help you get started when you have children. Remember, the lessons you teach them will have to guide them through a complicated society in what is rapidly becoming a perverse generation.

# TRAIN UP A CHILD

God's Word says, "Train up a child in the way he should go, even when he is old he will not depart from it" (Prov. 22:6). Unfortunately, Christians aren't immune to divorce, and neither are their children.

I am always mindful of the people I have counseled, because they mean so much to me. Often, as I think back over the years, God brings to mind those people who have been so special. I remember one couple who came as newlyweds—for the third time. No, they didn't come in for the third time. It was the third time they had been married—to each other. They had first gotten married in high school, secretly. When they finally told their parents about it, they were both asked to leave their homes.

They tried to make it on their own, but the odds were against them, and within a year they were separated and then divorced. Paul went into the army for two years, and Faye went home to finish high school.

In the service Paul began to write to Faye, and on leaves he and Faye began to date. She finished high school about the time Paul's tour in the army was up, and they were married for the second time.

At first they had no problems, but eventually the same old habits got them into financial trouble. They never knew how much they had in their checking account. Faye needed clothes so she charged them; Paul bought a new car—just the normal things that young couples do today. Their parents bailed them out a couple of times, but each time the situations got worse. Eventually they were divorced for a second time.

Paul earned his high school equivalency diploma and was determined to go to college. He was working his way through when he bumped into Faye again almost three years later during a school break. They began to see each other infrequently and within a year were dating regularly. Paul had become very active in a campus ministry and had committed his life to Christ. During a rally, Faye committed her life to Christ, and they decided to get married for the third time.

This time they realized they lacked the training to handle their finances properly and determined they would not commit the same mistakes again. In the Lord's timing, I was doing a seminar at the college on personal finances for students. Paul couldn't have been more excited if someone had given him a million dollars. The areas I discussed with the students were an exact parallel to what he and Faye had experienced twice before. They had come out of middle-class families that did everything for their children except teach them how to be adults. They tried to mimic their parents but lacked the resources to make it work.

I spent several sessions with Paul and Faye, during which I took them through the basics, from checkbook balancing to how to budget a (very) limited income. They learned quickly and enthusiastically because they both had seen the effect that poor money management could have on a marriage.

We met several times after they were married, just to be sure they had everything under control, which they did. They began to teach classes for young couples at their church with such startling results that their pastor asked them to take over the premarried and newlywed classes. The changes in the finances of the young couples they taught were directly measurable in a zero divorce rate over the next several years, and Paul and Faye's legacy extended even beyond their ministry there. Faye is now a full-time counselor with a large bank, where she helps restore the finances of couples with bad credit.

# 19 DECLINING CHRISTIANITY

Through the influence of the materialistic society in which we live, we have a declining rate of Christianity. Having Christian parents does not guarantee committed Christian children.

I do a great deal of traveling, and many times I'll get into a conversation with someone sitting next to me on an airplane. Eventually the conversation gets around to the subject that is most important to me: Jesus Christ. I'll ask, "Are you a Christian?" Conservatively, 90 percent of the people I ask say they are. It's interesting how some of them think people become Christians. Either their father used to be a pastor, they were baptized as a child, or their grandmother used to be a missionary. I often share with them, "Friend, you don't get to be a car by sitting in a garage, and you don't get to be a Christian by sitting in church."

You also don't get to be a Christian by growing up in a Christian family. Christian parents can influence their children a great deal, but the danger is that they will just learn the language. Then they'll be able to tell you what you want to hear, without it being real in their lives.

One of the things I have found with my children, and with others I've counseled over the years, is that there are signs and indicators God has given that reveal true Christianity. If children have no commitment to giving without parental pressure, it is either because they aren't saved or because they don't understand the lordship of Christ. Certainly early teaching is important, even critical, but at some point it must become *their* decision. When I find a Christian's offspring who doesn't give, I ask this question: Is he really saved, or is he only repeating what he was taught?

## FINANCES: AN INDICATOR

When it comes to youths, I believe you can measure the level of their commitment to the Lord in part by the way they handle their finances, especially how they respond to God's financial principles. Remember that obedience to God fluctuates sometimes and so will that of our children. It's the life patterns that provide the indicators. Also let me assure you that a slothful, indulgent child will almost always develop into a slothful, indulgent adult. The sooner you spot the faults, the sooner you can help correct them.

Children coming out of Christian families quite often see one thing and hear another. Parents are the best (or worst) models of Christianity their children will see. Remember what James said: "Prove yourselves doers of the word, and not merely hearers who delude themselves" (1:22).

Al and Carol became Christians about ten years into their marriage, though from different sides of the fence. Carol was of the charismatic persuasion and Al was a fundamentalist. He thought she was nuts and she thought he was unsaved. But the real losers in their frequent yelling matches were their children.

Carol came from a wealthy background where money was the equivalent of a person's value. Her father was the chairman of every board or committee in the church, and her mother ruled her father.

Al's parents were divorced while he was still in high school, and he grew up to be a "self-made" man who resisted any woman's hint at authority. Theirs was a situation ripe for Satan to exploit.

Their children were *sent* to church and Sunday school because Al wouldn't attend Carol's church, nor would he allow their children to attend. Often he wouldn't go to church because of a heated argument on Sunday morning. So he would drop off the kids and just drive around.

The impact that church made on their children was basically zero. They heard about love and understanding at Sunday school but witnessed warfare at home, much of it motivated by spiritual differences.

Carol began to make a habit of running home every time she and Al would have a fight. The kids were usually caught in the middle and were forced to side with one parent or the other. In the meantime, the grandparents also began to vie for the kids by buying them expensive presents while they were visiting.

As the children grew up, they became more and more difficult to control. Both Al and Carol realized they were wrong, but they were trapped by bitterness and pride.

At last, a Christian friend of Al's invited them to a weekend family conference where the topics were communications and finances. The weekend had a profound effect on both Al and Carol, and they rededicated their lives to the Lord.

In applying some of the principles they had learned, they decided to stop requiring that their two teenage sons give to the church, and they began regularly attending church as a family.

Their sons immediately stopped all giving and told their parents they would rather not even go to church anymore. The parents were stunned to discover the true spiritual condition of their children. It was all head knowledge and no heart knowledge. The parental examples spoke much louder than any pastor or Sunday school teacher.

Al and Carol had a long way to go to win back the hearts of their children before they became adults. Fortunately they woke up in time to have some influence while the children were still under their daily authority. Within five years they saw all of their children accept Jesus and commit to His service. The kids no longer required Mom or Dad to tell them to give. In fact, they challenged their parents to give more and spend less.

## WHERE DO YOU START?

Where should you start in teaching your children? First, I would like to offer three fundamental principles that are applicable to everyone, parents and children. These are condensed from my book titled *God's Guide through the Money Jungle*, part of the Youth Bible Study series.

1. *Teach your children that God owns everything by allowing them to see this principle in your lives.* Demonstrate that you're willing to put aside your own indulgences to meet needs in other people's lives. Begin to pray about the material needs you have and let God provide them without borrowing so that your children can see that God is real.

2. *Exercise self-discipline.* There's no way that parents can establish financial discipline in their children if they themselves are undisciplined.

In a practical way, this may be as simple as sharing your budget with your children to show them how you save to buy clothes, repair your car, or take vacations. Too often our children are led to believe that money really does grow on trees and all we have to do is pick some off when we need it. To allow your children to live this fantasy is to invite disaster when they're adults.

Parents need to practice moderation, regardless of their ability to generate income. God's instructions require that we exercise discipline in everything we do. It's easy to rationalize indulgence and lavishness under the "live like the King's kid" philosophy. If you believe that, look at the examples in God's Word. First, observe the King and see if He ever lived lavishly. Second, look at the men whom Christ poured His life into and see if they did. And third, look at the apostle Paul's example. You don't have to live in poverty to serve Christ, but self-discipline and moderation are rules.

3. *Teach your children that everybody needs to live on a budget.* It doesn't matter whether you make $8,000 a year or $800,000 a year; you need a budget.

A budget for children is a plan for managing their money as they make it. The simplest budget for a child has four parts: giving, spending, savings, and surplus. The plan I recommend to start with is 10 percent for giving, 40 percent for spending, 25 percent for long-term savings (college, cars, and the like), and 25 percent for surplus (a standby reserve fund).

The spending budget can be further divided according to the age and needs of each child. Obviously, the spending needs of an eight-year-old will be vastly different from those of a seventeen-year-old.

# 20  TRAINING CHILDREN AGES 1–10

Let's discuss some practical financial ideas for young children, ages one through ten. Normally, during the first ten years, the basic attitudes of your children are being formed. You're not going to change their basic personalities no matter what you do. But you can mold their character by reinforcing their strong points and correcting their flaws. The way they manage money is merely a measure of their strengths and weaknesses.

For young children, you need to assign some nonpaying jobs, such as cleaning their rooms, doing the dishes, and picking up their toys. As Proverbs 15:20 says, *"A wise son makes a father glad, but a foolish man despises his mother."* All children need some basic responsibilities for which they don't get paid. My children objected when I started implementing this philosophy in our family, admittedly a bit late. They believed they should get paid for everything they did. The point I tried to get across was that we're all part of a society and that each of us has things we *have* to do. I would usually point out that I didn't get paid for changing their diapers when they were young, and they don't get paid for taking out the garbage now.

You also should provide some paying jobs for your children— moving the lawn, cleaning the garage, washing the car, and so on. There are a variety of things you should pay your children to do, and you should pay them equitably, according to what you are able to afford.

When we lived in Tucker, Georgia (just outside Atlanta), we owned a house on a steep hill; in fact, if you stepped onto my front yard without baseball cleats on, you could end up in my backyard! So obviously, it was a tough lawn to mow. My oldest son was very com-pliant; whatever I asked him to do, he did it. When I said, "Please mow the lawn," he mowed it, and whatever I paid him was okay, within reason.

My second son questioned everything. (If you ever have a child who asks "Why?" all the time, then you'll understand.) He had ninety-nine ways to use the word *why*. When he turned twelve, he became eligible to mow our lawn. The first thing he asked was, "How much?" I said, "I'll pay you $7." He replied, "It's not worth it. I'm not going to mow that lawn for $7." I said, "That's okay, but that's the only way you have to earn money. If you don't do it, you don't get any money. Do you understand that?" He said, "Sure, Dad, but I'm not going to mow that lawn for $7."

So I went to a friend who had a son about the same age and negotiated with him to mow the lawn for $7. He was there within five minutes, mowing my lawn. Every week after that, my son mowed our lawn. He decided if it was worth it to his friend, it was worth it to him.

## BE FAIR, BUT FIRM

You need to be fair with your children but also firm. There are some simple rules to observe. According to Matthew 10:10, "The worker is worthy of his support." I believe that's true with our children as well. If you want to train your children to be good employees, you must take on the role of an employer. Therefore, you have to establish some principles that any reasonable employer would.

1. *Pay them only for jobs that are completed.* I told my children from the beginning that they wouldn't get 90 percent of the money

for 90 percent of the job. I would pay them 100 percent of the money for 100 percent of the job. In other words, if they didn't finish, they wouldn't get paid. Why? Because no employer is going to pay them for a partially finished job. What if an employee decided, "I don't want to work five days a week, so I'll only work four days." Do you think an employer would agree? Hardly so; most employers expect a full week's work. It would be like a car painter saying, "I don't like painting a whole car. I'll just paint half of it, so just pay me for the half I paint." It just doesn't work that way. As Proverbs 12:11 says, "He who tills his land will have plenty of bread, but he who pursues worthless things lacks sense."

2. *Pay for quality work.* Scripture says, "Whatever you do, do your work heartily, as for the Lord rather than for men" (Col. 3:23). I tried to convey to my children that they need to be the best they can be. That doesn't mean they need to be the best in the world; they may not have that ability. It means they should be the best they are capable of being. If Christian employees would manifest two biblical characteristics, there would never be an unemployed Christian. First, give honor to the authority over them, doing everything possible to promote that authority; second, do the best job possible within their abilities.

3. *Pay fairly, within your budget, but don't overpay because you can afford it.* I have a good friend who has lived to regret not heeding this advice. When his children went to work for him, he started them out at about $8 an hour. By the time they graduated from high school, they were making nearly $20 an hour! When they went to college, he bought each of them a brand-new automobile. Then, when they graduated from college, he decided they were on their own and were

no longer his responsibility. Unfortunately, he had preconditioned their expectations. They had made $20 an hour mowing lawns and drove new cars in college. What employer would be able to match that, allowing them to maintain that standard of living? None, he found out. His children still shift from job to job, looking for that executive position that will match their expectations and enable them to live the life they have come to expect.

You need to be very careful that you don't overpay. Remember, the principles that you're trying to build into your children's lives have to sustain them throughout their lifetimes. So pay fairly, but don't overpay.

4. *Use visual reinforcement, especially for young children.* Most parents find that a chart on the back of a door works very well. Not every child is motivated by charts, but most are. My second son couldn't have cared less about charts. He would say, "Forget the stars. How much does it pay?"

Most young children, however, are motivated by praise and rewards, and charts serve that function well. One thing children will demand is honesty. If you say a star represents a job well done, be sure you're faithful to that rule. Almost always one child, especially a girl, will be the guardian of the rules. Children will be sure to let you know if you're not true to your word, and well they should. If you don't really mean it, don't say it.

5. *Teach your children "sharing" principles from God's Word.* One thing I encourage you to avoid is the "quarter-in-the-plate" syndrome. Many Christian parents fall into that trap. The offering plate is coming around in church, and they give their children a quarter to drop in. That means absolutely nothing to most of them. They didn't earn the

money, so it didn't cost them anything to give it away; therefore, giving becomes a religious ritual. I would encourage you to avoid that. It's best for your children to give only if it costs them something.

Help your children get involved with the needs of people. Helping them invest directly in the lives of other people, particularly the poor, is what works best with most children. Once they see that giving is God's way of sharing a surplus where others have a lack, it will become real to them. I know children who have supported orphans for several years, and they still get letters from those they were helping. This helps children understand the purpose as well as the principle of giving. It isn't just dropping money in a plate. It's being involved in the lives of other people. Once a child is committed to that concept, nobody has to force him or her to give.

If you must force your children to give, somewhere along the way they'll get big enough to stop. If they give because of God's conviction and His Word, nobody will ever talk them out of it. I have met four- and five-year-old children who were committed to giving funds they had earned and felt it a privilege to do so. Some were able to give only a dime or a quarter, but they gave to meet the needs of another. A quarter isn't much in America, but in Mexico it will buy a day's worth of food. As Paul said, "At this present time your abundance being a supply for their need, so that their abundance also may become a supply for your need, that there may be equality" (2 Cor. 8:14).

6. *Teach your children to save.* Proverbs 21:20 says, "There is precious treasure and oil in the dwelling of the wise, but a foolish man swallows it up."

It's hard to understand why so many parents who have had bitter experiences with debt, including divorce, fail to teach their children how to avoid it. In reality, any parent can discourage debt simply by encouraging saving. After all, we need things (kids do too) and must either save or borrow to get them.

While teaching a group of seminary students on the biblical principles of managing money, I found myself counseling virtually every free minute. These students were about to graduate into careers as pastors and missionaries, and they were deep in debt. Most had student loans that stretched back seven or eight years. Others had credit card debts, car loans, bank loans, and family loans. Without realizing it, most of these potential Christian leaders had doomed their careers and marriages through excessive borrowing. Few churches would be able to pay salaries sufficient to meet their needs, and virtually no mission groups could.

A young man named Jeremy shared that his father had encouraged him to start saving at a very early age and promised to match his saving dollar for dollar if he wouldn't touch it for ten years. He worked the normal kids' jobs: a paper route, summer work, washing cars, and so on. He had used some of his savings to purchase a pressure cleaner for sidewalks while in high school and started going door to door, cleaning driveways and sidewalks. After that, he was self-employed.

By the time he started college, he owned a car and had over $20,000 in savings. He supplemented his savings by working at his business during vacations and summers. His father paid for one-half of his college expenses, and he paid the other half.

When Jeremy graduated from college and entered seminary, he sold his cleaning business for $25,000 and used $5,000 to purchase a parking lot striping machine. So he entered seminary debt-free and with $20,000 in savings. He again supplemented his savings by painting stripes on small parking lots. That business grew to employ four other students. He was about to graduate from seminary and had sold his latest business for $40,000. The only difference between Jeremy and the vast majority of other students was that his father had introduced him to sound biblical principles of handling money at an early age. It's as Proverb 22:6 says: "Train up a child in the way he should go, even when he is old he will not depart from it."

# 21   TRAINING CHILDREN AGES 11–16

When your children are between the ages of eleven and sixteen, you need to increase their level of understanding about finances. There are a few basic principles that parents need to concentrate on during this transition period to adulthood.

1. *There's no such thing in God's economy as an allowance.* An allowance implies money given by a parent but disassociated from performance. Look around any university in America today and you'll see the product of "allowing" parents. What you really need to teach your teenagers is responsibility. As the apostle Paul said, "For even when we were with you, we used to give you this order: if anyone is not willing to work, then he is not to eat, either" (2 Thess. 3:10). Obviously, you don't want to withhold food from a sixteen-year-old. But you can withhold your car.

So many times parents indulge because they love, but indulgence is the exact opposite of real love; *real* love does what is best for the other person, regardless of the difficulties for you.

It's an interesting phenomenon that children grow up resenting a parent who was too harsh, but they also resent a parent who was too lenient. I have heard many mothers say they don't understand why their children resent them later in life when all they ever did was give, give, give. That is *exactly* the problem. They buffered their children rather than trained them.

2. *Have a very strict performance code for work your teenagers do.* In our seminar on biblical principles for operating a business, one of the principles we teach is what happens when employers don't establish definitive standards for employees. The employees don't know what is expected.

We need to establish standards for our children, including timeliness, dependability, attitude, and honor. These are the standards by which God evaluates success or failure.

I have a friend who uses his business to provide job opportunities for young people just starting out. He says he is continually amazed at the lack of responsibility on the part of many young people, even from Christian homes. He expects no special job knowledge from the teenagers he hires, but he has two absolute standards: be at work on time every day and maintain a good attitude.

If they adhere to these standards and *try*, he will train them thoroughly. He told me the story of Greg, a young man he hired. Greg came from a broken home and had been raised by a Christian grandmother. When Greg came to his company through a work-study program at his high school, he was enthusiastic about a chance to work at something with a future.

Greg proved to be bright and enthusiastic but on the undisciplined side. He was prompt and dependable for the first couple of weeks but then began to be late periodically and call in with a variety of excuses for why he couldn't come to work.

My friend suffered through Greg's bad habits until summer because Greg showed such promise when he *was* working. After being disciplined, he would improve for a while and then lapse back into his bad habits.

During the summer break, Greg was employed full-time. But he was often tardy and periodically just didn't show up at all. Each time he was apologetic, but the cycle continued. His grandmother told my friend, "He loves his job, but that boy just can't get out of bed in the mornings." She asked him to please not fire Greg. "He wants to work; he's just never had a real job before."

Finally, in desperation, my friend sent one of his supervisors by Greg's home in the mornings to get him up and in to work. As normal, Greg was ready the first few days but then lapsed into sleeping late. The supervisor told Greg's grandmother, "You put a full pitcher of water in the refrigerator every night. I'll get him up."

The next day when he came, Greg was still asleep. He took the pitcher of very cold water and went into Greg's room. He said, "Greg, you going to work today?" "Yes, sir," Greg replied, "in a minute," and he went back to sleep. His sleep was interrupted by two quarts of near-freezing water.

He fussed and fumed while he was getting dried off and dressed for work. His grandmother cackled, "I'll leave that mess for you to clean up tonight!"

The next day the whole routine repeated itself. The third day when the supervisor came to get Greg, he asked Greg's grandmother if he was still in bed. She said, "Well, he got up, but I believe he's asleep again." When she opened the refrigerator door to get the pitcher, Greg heard it and leaped out of bed, fully clothed!

As time passed, Greg became one of the most valued employees this company had. He is now a plant manager with children of his own. You can be certain that he is teaching his children to do their work well, on time, and with dependability. Greg often says to his sons, "If a stranger loved me enough to hold me accountable for my work habits, I surely can do as much for you boys."

Remember that the earlier you start instilling the right habits in your children, the easier it is. It's *never* too late, but the earlier the better. "Correct your son, and he will give you comfort; he will also delight your soul" (Prov. 29:17).

3. *Reward extra effort.* If your children are excellent at what they do and put forth extra effort, they should be rewarded for doing a superior job.

Paul said, "The hard-working farmer ought to be the first to receive his share of the crops" (2 Tim. 2:6). It's important that your children understand the "no-work, no-pay" principle. But it is just as important that they understand the "better-work, better-pay" principle.

You can begin to teach this principle even at the youngest ages by acknowledging when a child puts out extra effort. That does not mean equal performance necessarily. Each child has differing abilities and what may be extra effort to one may be coasting to another. You need to be able to evaluate when a child is trying harder.

One of our sons tended to be a perfectionist, even as a small child. Picking up his clothes and toys and cleaning his room were natural for him. As a result, he was praised and rewarded. Any parent who wouldn't do so would have to be a little crazy. Another son tended to be messy and rarely, if ever, noticed his disorder. When he took the time and effort to pick up his things or clean his room, he was looking for praise (or money). The more often we did so, the more normal it became for him. From time to time we raised our standards for rewards. It probably took three years before his "norm" reached the other son's low average. But had we never rewarded him in the beginning, the process would never have started.

It is effort, not skill level, you must measure and commend.

4. *Stick to your convictions.* Don't be swayed into lowering your standards simply because you have Christian friends who do. Sometimes the most conflicting value system you'll find is in a Christian school. When your children are in contact with other children from Christian homes and find their values aren't the same, they will challenge your rules.

Unfortunately, many Christian parents don't pay by any performance standards and buy their children virtually anything they want, anytime they want it. The sad thing is that they actually believe this demonstrates love. The tendency is to be swayed into doing the same thing for your children. Don't compound their error. Remember that God's Word says, "He who withholds his rod hates his son, but he who loves him disciplines him diligently" (Prov. 13:24). Discipline is not for punishment. It is to set boundaries for your children. Within those boundaries they are secure.

One of the major difficulties children have today is that they are being asked to make adult decisions before they're ready. The secular world makes an almost unbelievable array of temptations available to them at a very young age. God has established the parents to be their buffers. Set your standards according to God's Word and stick to them.

Many times I will volunteer to teach classes at various Christian schools just to get a feel for where Christian families are in the training of their children. I have to be honest and say it's rather depressing, with a few exceptions.

I like to take surveys of how these kids have been trained. I usually ask these questions (with the answers I'm given following in parentheses): How many are assigned chores that take an hour a week or more? (about 10 percent); How many have to earn their allowances? (about 10 percent); How many receive allowances of $5 a week or more? (about 50 percent); How many believe their parents should control how they spend their money? (about 2 percent); How many believe their parents handle their money well, based on family arguments? (about 10 percent); How many would like to be like their parents? (about 10 percent).

This is by no means a scientific survey, but it does demonstrate that parents are neglecting a fundamental area of education for their children. If you don't set your own standards and stick to them, your children will be the losers.

5. *Teach teenagers the principle of budgeting.* Like Dad and Mom, teenagers should know well the condition of their herds and their flocks (see Prov. 27:23). In other words, they should know where their money goes *before* they spend it.

It is important to me that my children get my counsel before they get married. A mistake in choosing the right partner can result in grief for a lot of people, myself included. My oldest son came to me and shared that he wanted to get married. After getting to know his fiancée I said, "I approve of your choice; she's a great girl. But before you get married, I want to see a budget that shows what you will earn and how you plan to spend it for the first year." I never doubted his ability to budget in his own family because he budgeted his money well when he lived at home. It was a sparse but workable budget, and they made it.

It's sad to see how many young couples don't make it because they get married with no financial training at all. If you think the schools will do this training for you, think again. For years I tried to get Christian schools to establish a basic home finance class and make it mandatory for graduation. Even after writing the curriculum for it, I found virtually no takers.

Since it wasn't a part of the "approved" curriculum by the accreditation groups, they couldn't spare the time. I wondered whatever happened to God's accreditation system. I have since taken the material into homes and churches, where it has been enthusiastically adopted. I'll share a few of the ideas in the next chapter.

Don't expect your children to jump up and down with joy when you begin to enforce financial discipline, including a budget. I remember when my strong-willed (hardheaded) son was about twelve years old and I started him on a budget. He had been used to spending his money, which he earned, pretty much the way he desired. I knew a budget was in his best interest, but he didn't see it that way at all.

We were about three weeks into the budgeting process, which included about half of his money going into savings, when he came into my office one day and said, "Dad, this is not a very democratic way to run a family." I said, "You're right, son. You don't live in a democracy in our home; you live in a benevolent dictatorship."

He mumbled and grumbled from time to time because he couldn't stand to think about unspent money. But he survived and we did too.

Later he joined the Marine Corps Reserve, where he went through boot camp training and then through a year of electronics training. I was speaking in California, where he was stationed, and I decided to drive out to see him one Sunday afternoon.

You need to realize that the whole time my son was living at home, he was always arguing. "Dad, this isn't right, that isn't right, I don't agree with that." Whatever rule I established, he wanted to stretch it. He would stretch it until he reached my boundaries, and then he would back off.

But that day in California, he said something that made all the grief we had endured worthwhile. He said, "Dad, I never told you how much I appreciate what you've done for me. You established discipline in my life that I don't see in most of the other guys I'm around. They cry and they complain, and then they wash out because they've never learned to discipline themselves." It was worth all the years of struggling to see the end results in his life. It was worse on me than it was on him, though he probably would not agree with that at all.

As I said earlier, a general guide in budgeting for your children is very simple. The first part of their income should go to God. The question is often asked, "Should I force my children to tithe?" I personally would not. At ages one to ten, I would encourage them and tell them to do it, because at this point you're developing the principles in their lives. At eleven to sixteen, it should be their choice, because you need to find out whether they have come to agree with what you've been teaching them.

About 25 percent of their earnings should be put into a savings account for short-term use. The next 25 percent should be saved for long-term needs, and about 40 percent should be theirs to spend according to an approved budget.

By the way, I encourage parents not to just drop these principles on their kids. The first step is to put them into your own life and then start sharing them with your children.

I had a young woman call me one time after a seminar. She said, "You have ruined my life."

"How have I ruined your life?" I asked. At that seminar I had been talking about paying for college education, and I shared with the group what we do with our children. We pay half and they pay half.

She said, "You've ruined my life. I came home on spring break from college, and my dad said, 'You can't go back until you earn half of your tuition.'"

I said, "You tell him he's absolutely wrong. Number one, I didn't tell him that was a biblical principle. I said it was what *we* did. Second, he can't drop that on you during spring break."

You must start such a plan at least ten years before the first child enters college. You can't just decide to implement it on an impulse. As Paul said, "Fathers, do not provoke your children to anger, but bring them up in the discipline and instruction of the Lord" (Eph. 6:4).

Try to make your children a part of the planning process in your home, not the object of it. Share your budget with your children, just the same way they must share theirs with you.

# 22 TRAINING CHILDREN AGES 17–20

Some of you reading this book probably don't have teenagers yet, much less young adults. In fact, some of you probably fit into this age-group yourselves. That's all right. We have all been seventeen to twenty at one time or another, and all of our children will be. This is a crucial age because these are the transition years to adulthood.

By this time the basics of personal finances *must* be understood and applied, or the mistakes of past generations will be repeated. I would like to present the essentials that children should be taught while still under their parents' authority.

1. *Work/vocation.* The essential step is to determine the personality, skills, and gifts that God has given to each of your children. In our generation, it is not abnormal for young men and women to graduate from college and have no idea what they want to do vocationally. All too often they take any job that is available, only to find out later that they dislike the career field. Usually it's because personality and career field are mismatched.

Marsha was an example of this mismatch between personality and vocation. She had studied accounting in college and graduated with good grades. She took a job with an auditing company and found that she dreaded the daily routine. The only part of her job she enjoyed was when she could work on problem solving.

Her father, an accountant for a Big Eight firm, sent her to a vocational counselor, who discovered the cause of her discomfort. She had a creative personality that required frequent change and challenging tasks. The last thing she needed was routine functions. He recommended that she go to law school (a longtime desire of hers) and study investigative law. She now is an investigator with a government securities agency and loves it. Her father was wise enough to point her in the right direction.

The next step is to help your older teenagers gather some career facts. Even if you can't determine for them the exact career field they should get involved in, usually you can help them avoid the ones where they wouldn't fit. Perhaps the simplest way is to talk to Christians in those careers. Ask fundamental questions such as (1) What kind of education is required? (2) What training is required? (3) What personality type performs best? (4) What hours do you work?

My daughter had always wanted to be a veterinarian, primarily because she loved animals. Later in college, she changed her mind and decided that she wanted to be a physician. After many long conversations with friends of mine who are medical doctors, her career field changed to psychology. She found that she wasn't willing to pay the price (in time) that a physician pays. She was able to make that decision without wasting several years of schooling simply by talking with others who had already gone that route.

2. *Self-determination.* Within limits, from the time your children are about sixteen to seventeen years old, you need to allow them to make their own financial decisions. Certainly the decisions you allow will vary by age and personality, but the more opportunities you allow now, the clearer picture you'll have of what they will do later.

**Clothes.** As any mother of teenagers knows, it's hard to select the clothes that you can afford and that they will wear. At some point you need to shift the decision-making process over to them.

I suggest allowing your teenagers to select their own wardrobe based on a quarterly clothes budget. Obviously, the parents need to establish some fundamental rules regarding modesty, price, and style. But the decision about where to shop and what to buy should be the teenagers'. There are some hazards in yielding this authority, but you need to bear in mind that, as parents, you are raising future adults who will eventually have the sole right to make these decisions. It's always enlightening to see your earlier evaluations revealed in your children's buying habits. It often helps parents focus on their children's weak areas, as well as their strengths.

I recall the example of two teenagers whose parents decided to give them total responsibility for buying their clothes. They spent several hours discussing where to find the best buys, how to pick quality clothes, and so on. Then one fateful summer day, Mom dropped them off in the shopping mall with about $200 each to buy school clothes.

The older son, about sixteen and very conservative, bought exactly what they had discussed: tennis shoes, jeans, shirts, and underwear. The younger son, about thirteen and very strong willed, bought a couple of pairs of socks, a silk-screened T-shirt, and a very expensive skateboard. Later that evening during their family time, his father said, "Rick, we gave you the right and responsibility to make your own decisions about what clothes to buy. Just remember, no more clothes money for at least three months."

Rick replied, "Don't you worry, Dad. I've got plenty of clothes for school."

Over the next couple of weeks, Rick succeeded in virtually destroying his pants, shirts, and shoes practicing on his new skateboard. About three days before school was to start, Rick came downstairs to where his dad was reading and said, "Dad, I have a problem. I can't go to school like this." He showed his tennis shoes with his toes sticking out of them.

Rick's dad replied, "Oh, that's really a shame. You're right. You can't go to school like that." And with that, he got some black electrical tape and wrapped it around Rick's shoes. After three months of wearing ragged jeans and holey shoes, Rick got the idea that his parents were serious. His dad had proved that he had some lessons to learn about money, and the next time he received his clothing budget, he bought what he needed.

**Cars.** Whether or not to allow your son or daughter to have a car in high school is a major decision, even if he or she buys it. But to provide a car and cover all the expenses usually works to the long-term detriment of most teenagers. Obviously there are exceptions, but in general, cars are a luxury and an indulgence for students. Too often they're given to keep the kids out of the parents' hair.

If you're going to allow your teenagers to use your vehicles, I would suggest some basic rules:

- They should pay for their own insurance.
- They should pay a portion of the maintenance and upkeep. I suggest a usage rate of five cents per mile.
- They should provide their own gas and oil.
- They should clean the car after every use or at least once per week.
- They should pay all of their traffic violations, and driving privileges should be suspended for serious violations.

Just the fact that your teenager pays for his or her own car expenses is not justification for giving him or her free rein. A car is a large expense and a distraction that costs many high school students their futures. Remember how much trouble cars are in your life, and help your children avoid trouble. They may get irritated, but they'll get over it, I promise.

3. *Checking account.* Without hesitation, I can say that by age sixteen, your children should be using and maintaining their own checking accounts.

In preparation, I would encourage you to work through the checking account section of this book with them to be sure they understand how to balance their accounts. Since most teenagers can get along without checking accounts, most never have them. Those who do often end up with a big mess in which the parents pay for overdrafts and usually cancel the account. That is *not* the answer to poor management.

Remember that you're not raising children; you're raising future adults, and in our society, checking accounts are a fact of life. Don't let your children leave home without the basic skills for survival. Teach your daughter to maintain and balance her checkbook properly, and one day your future son-in-law will fall down and call you blessed.

A small bribe in this area often helps motivate teenagers. In other words, promise them a financial reward for maintaining their checking accounts perfectly.

I would suggest a bonus of $100 (or whatever your budget can handle) for maintaining and balancing their checking account for a year. I would further encourage you to let them spend this money as they see fit (within reason) to give them additional incentive.

4. *Credit cards.* Contrary to popular opinion, I do recommend allowing children to use credit cards. Remember, credit cards are *not* the problem. It is the *misuse* of credit cards that creates the problems.

I personally believe it would be better if young couples didn't have access to so much credit. But in a society where the whole economy runs on debt, credit is a fact of life. So it's best to teach your children how to manage and control it, not vice versa.

I would suggest allowing teenagers to have credit cards in their names at about age seventeen or eighteen. The rules for using the card should be clear, written, and absolute.

- The card can be used *only* for budgeted items—clothes, gas, tires, and so on.
- The account has to be paid in full each month—no exceptions.
- The *first* month the account isn't paid, take the card back and destroy it.

I have seen parents establish these rules and then fail to enforce them because of a sad tale of circumstances told by their teenager. To fail to keep the rules is to invite more violations. If you're not committed to enforcing the rules of credit, don't let your teenagers have a credit card. All you'll do is encourage debt. Debt is a great temptation that is virtually irresistible without stern control, as thousands of divorced young couples will attest.

My record for teenage credit card debt was set by a young woman about eighteen when she went off to college at a state university, fresh out of a Christian school.

Her father didn't want her to get caught without money if her car broke down, so he arranged to have a credit card issued in her name. Unfortunately, she had no experience with such devices and misused the card a little. In fact, she became the most popular girl on campus because she loaned her card out liberally.

At the end of her second month of college, the bills began to appear on the statement, which came to her parents' home. Her father obviously thought the bills were a mistake and complained to the credit card company.

When this father, a financial planner, found out what his daughter had done, he canceled her card—but not before she had allowed $11,000 to be charged to her credit card. It's no smarter to give a teenager a credit card without training than it is to give a baby a hand grenade. Eventually they will both discover what it was made to do, with about the same effect.

5. *Personal expenses.* The question is often asked, "Should we charge our children for their room and board if they're working?" This is a matter of judgment on the part of the parents. In general, I believe you should not charge a high-school-age child room and board. Obviously, the needs of the family must be taken into consideration. If a financial need exists, it may be necessary for teenagers to contribute to the family's income. I have seen many such situations and rarely witnessed a detrimental effect on the child. In fact, usually the exact opposite was true, and the teenager reflected maturity far beyond his or her peers.

A widow named Pam was left with three children ages ten, twelve, and sixteen when her husband committed suicide while suffering with terminal cancer. Because of the suicide, his insurance was voided and she received virtually nothing. She had few marketable skills, so she took up sewing at home. Her daughter, a high school junior, got a job in the school office during weekdays and a babysitting job on weekends.

By her senior year, she had moved from the school office to a local attorney's office as part of a school-work program. He was so impressed by her maturity and work ethic that he sponsored her to go to a court stenographer's school when she graduated from high school.

She later did all of his personal courtroom reporting and was earning a salary in excess of $20,000 a year. Within three years, he had helped her start her own transcription business, and at twenty-four she was managing an office with four transcription secretaries. She matured through her problems. Unfortunately, not all teenagers do.

Even with children who are out of school and working while living at home, the decision about charging them room and board is not simple. In great part, it will depend on the needs and attitude of the child. Even if the parents don't need the money, I believe it's a good practice to charge working children. They need the accountability that paying their own expenses can provide. You can always put the money in a savings account and give it back to them later when they move out on their own.

6. *Adult decisions.* Ideally what we would like to achieve with our children is to prepare them totally to make the financial decisions they will be facing as adults. But most of them won't be trained to make decisions such as which house to buy or how much and what type of life insurance to purchase.

The best way to prepare them, outside of actually buying those items, is to simulate the needs. In other words, do role-playing in which they make decisions similar to those they will make on their own. I have done this many times with high school classes in which I pair kids into teams to learn basic financial planning. I assign each team (usually a boy and girl) a job and related salary. For instance, one team is a schoolteacher making $45,000 annually; another is a dentist making $140,000; another is an assembly-line worker making $30,000; another is a two-income family making $90,000.

Each team is required to select the items for each area of their budget—from houses to vacations—with the applicable costs, such as down payments, monthly payments, utilities, and repairs. Their task is to fit what they select into their available funds each month.

After just one week of budgeting, most teams are looking to trade in houses, cars, clothes, and vacations—all in light of how much they cost compared to available funds. By about the fourth session, they have become seasoned budgeters. With your children, find a system that works and use it.

## SUMMARY

We are called by God to be the teachers of our children. It is *not* an option. It is a biblical admonition. "The rod and reproof give wisdom, but a child who gets his own way brings shame to his mother" (Prov. 29:15).

We are not going to be held responsible for their decisions. Each person is held accountable individually. However, we will be held accountable for their instruction and training.

There are three basic principles that are applicable to all children. These should always be foremost in their training.

- Your children need to understand God's principles too. "Where there is no vision, the people are unrestrained, but happy is he who keeps the law" (Prov. 29:18).
- Love your children, but don't coddle them. "For whom the LORD loves He reproves, even as a father corrects the son in whom he delights" (Prov. 3:12).
- Allow your children to fail. "A worker's appetite works for him, for his hunger urges him on" (Prov. 16:26).

Remember that some of life's most valuable lessons are learned because of trying and failing. Love your children enough to allow them to fail while they're still in your home.

# PART FOUR

# TEN KEYS TO SUCCESSFUL INVESTING

# INTRODUCTION

The most important thing to remember is that it's wrong to invest just for the sake of making money. Making money should be a by-product of doing what God has called you to do. Also remember that peace does not come through the accumulation of material possessions; if it did, the wealthiest people in the world would be the most at peace. Instead, they're often frustrated and miserable. True peace comes only from God.

Another important principle to remember when considering any type of investing is that we are to be stewards—literally, managers of another's property. More specifically, we are the managers of God's property. It's good to recall what Paul said to Timothy: "For we have brought nothing into the world, so we cannot take anything out of it either" (1 Tim. 6:7). Remember, it's not how much you accumulate that's important; it's how it's being used.

## FIND THE RIGHT BALANCE

To allow material assets to erode through bad management is not good stewardship. It's a sign of slothfulness. But if you simply multiply and store them without purpose, you'll be guilty of hoarding, just as the rich fool did in Luke 12.

Investing is *not* unscriptural. In fact, in the parable of the talents recorded in Matthew 25:14–30, God gave to each of the stewards according to his ability and directed each to manage his portion well. One was given five talents, one was given three talents, and one was given one talent. Each was rewarded or punished according to his stewardship.

As you learn to invest money according to God's principles, you'll find that God will increase your opportunity to help other people. That is, in reality, the real purpose of investing: to increase your assets so you can serve God more fully. If you do as the rich fool did and tear down your barns to build larger ones, then expect God to deal with you as He did with the rich fool when He said, "This very night your soul is required of you; and now who will own what you have prepared?" (Luke 12:20).

## PURPOSES FOR INVESTING

A legitimate purpose of any investment program is to help your family achieve greater security. This can include investing to provide for your children's education, to provide a family inheritance, to provide for retirement, and the like. But there are also many nonscriptural reasons for investing: greed, indulgence, and covetousness, to name a few.

No single financial plan will fit every family. Unfortunately, today many financial planners tend to lump everybody into one mold. I believe in using financial advisers, and I encourage you to use them also. These include professionals in areas such as law, accounting, and financial planning. The key is to use them as sources of expertise, not as gurus. They can provide alternatives, suggestions, and expert advice, but ultimately the decisions must be yours.

There are basically two types of financial advisers. One gives advice and charges a fee for it. The other sells financial products in the process of giving advice. I consider the latter category more of a salesperson than a counselor. Salespeople have a place in the planning process, particularly in selecting investments, but they should not be used as primary counsel. Eventually, they're going to sell you the product they represent. Obviously, they believe in their products and rightly so, but diversity, as prescribed in Ecclesiastes 11:2, requires a much broader array of investments than one salesperson usually offers.

Even though every family's needs in the area of investing are different, there are certain common principles that can provide a solid foundation for anybody. I hesitate to label anything by number because it may take the rest of your life to implement the first two. Nevertheless, I have tried to distill the basic investing principles into ten keys or guidelines. If you'll read and apply these to your own financial plans, your investment decisions will be much clearer.

# 23 KEY #1: FORMULATE CLEAR-CUT INVESTMENT GOALS

No one should invest without having an ultimate purpose for the money. You may be laying money aside for education or retirement, but you should have an ultimate, clear-cut financial goal. I'd like to briefly discuss some realistic goals.

**Retirement Goal.** There is nothing wrong with retirement planning, provided that it's kept in balance. But in our society today, an eighteen-year-old goes out looking for a job with a good retirement plan. Many people look forward to retirement only because they hate the jobs they're in.

You should be where you can serve God best. If you are, retirement becomes less of an issue. Obviously, since you may not be able to do the same work at sixty-five or seventy that you're able to do at twenty-five or thirty, you may need to lay money aside to supplement your income later. In fact, retirement savings can allow you to volunteer for a Christian organization without the need for a salary.

The long-range goal of retirement will vary depending on the age and income of every individual. If you're thirty-five years old, your total perspective should be long-range growth and flexibility (diversity) of investments. The amount you will need to invest per month or year is significantly less than someone at age forty-five.

This same rule is true regardless of the long-range financial goal (retirement, education, and so forth). The longer the time period in which to plan, the less initial money it takes. However, different criteria apply to long-range investing—including hedging against inflation, depression, and financial collapse. Therefore, the actual investments you would select for retirement in forty years are different from those you might select for retirement in, say, ten years.

We'll review some actual investments later, but suffice it to say that a Treasury bill, paying 7 percent, may fit perfectly the retirement plan for a sixty-five-year-old widow but be totally inappropriate for a thirty-year-old attorney. Certainly, that would be true for the investments of any age-group.

According to the Social Security Administration, the average sixty-five-year-old man in America is worth about $100. In other words, if he cashed out all his assets and liquidated all his liabilities, he would be worth about $100.

Proverbs 6:6–8 says, "Go to the ant, O sluggard, observe her ways and be wise, which, having no chief, officer or ruler, prepares her food in the summer and gathers her provision in the harvest." These are the harvest years of your life. Remember that the winter years are coming.

**Preservation Goal.** Let's assume that you have inherited $100,000 and that you want to preserve that money for a particular purpose at a later date—perhaps education, retirement, or charitable donation. A couple starting out with $100,000 will have a different plan than a couple starting out at zero. A couple starting out at zero must first develop a surplus and then look for investments to help it grow. The couple with a $100,000 windfall should look first to preservation of the assets. I recall what Will Rogers once said: "I am not concerned so much with the return *on* my money, as I am with the return *of* my money." Typically the investment program for a onetime windfall will be very conservative. The goal is not to maximize the growth but rather minimize the losses and achieve a reasonable return.

Such is also the case for those who can put away sizable amounts from their current incomes. Doctors are a good example. The majority of money that most doctors have accumulated was earned through their primary profession: medicine. Most of what they lose is through speculative investments. The plan that most doctors need should be focused on the preservation of capital, with a reasonable degree of growth, to keep the value of their money current. They do not need high-risk investments.

**Education Goal.** Unlike those who are trying to preserve a windfall, a family with their children's education in mind must think more in terms of growth, again depending on the amount available to invest and the duration it can be invested.

Let's assume, for instance, that a couple can put aside $1,000 a year for the education of their children, who will reach college age in approximately ten years. The $10,000 they can save may not educate one child, much less two or three. So they're going to have to take some additional risks to achieve the growth they need.

The principle we'll be dealing with continually is the principle called "risk versus return." The higher rate of return you need, the greater degree of risk you will have to assume. There's an old cliché that says, "When a deal sounds too good to be true, it usually is." There are no free lunches.

**Income Goal.** A couple entering retirement and looking for maximum income to live on likely will have this fourth objective. They need income, but they also must be concerned with the preservation of their assets. Once their needed income level is met, other assets can be invested to offset inflation. Let's assume that a couple is approaching retirement, and they have $8,000 a year coming in through Social Security, but they know it's going to cost them $15,000 a year to live. Their primary concern is selecting investments that can earn $7,000 a year.

The risk they must assume is determined by the $7,000 income they need. If they have $100,000 and need a 7 percent return, they will probably be able to use very secure investments such as Treasury bills. But if they have only $50,000, T-bills won't do it. They'll need a 14 percent return, or at least as high as possible. So they're going to have to take some additional risks. The more they know about investing, the lower the risk will be.

**Growth Goal.** Everyone would like to have his or her investments grow. A growth strategy means there is minimal immediate need for the funds but a sizable future need. Carried to the extreme, this strategy is called "get rich quick," in which case it is unscriptural. As Proverbs 28:22 says, "A man with an evil eye hastens after wealth and does not know that want will come upon him."

A growth goal should be the strategy of someone fifty years of age who is able to save $1,000 a year toward retirement. The short period of time (fifteen years) and the limited funds ($1,000 a year) dictate an aggressive growth strategy.

This also would be the case of our couple with $10,000 to educate their children. They need an aggressive strategy that leans more toward risk taking than preservation.

**Tax Shelter Goal.** The sixth and final goal in investing is tax sheltering. Tax sheltering is very complex. In fact, for all intents and purposes, the federal government, through changes in the tax laws, virtually has shut down tax shelters other than depreciation and interest for the average investor. As I said before, it is often taught that paying interest is a good tax shelter. That is an old wives' tale. When you pay interest to save income tax, you lose and the lender gains.

However, depreciation and investment tax credits can be legitimate tax shelters. But an important principle to remember is that when you "defer" income tax through depreciation, you eventually must recapture it. Most tax shelters don't really eliminate income tax; they only defer it to a later time.

For instance, if you put money into a retirement plan such as an IRA, it is an excellent tax shelter. But you don't avoid the income taxes on your retirement funds. You delay them and are taxed later at a lower rate (hopefully) when you retire.

When you claim depreciation on rental property, you do not avoid paying income taxes. You defer them until a later period. When the property is sold, all of the depreciation you claimed can be recaptured in income taxes. The only exception is if you use the property as a charitable gift; then you can claim a charitable deduction for the fair market value of the property and will not have to repay the depreciated portion. (Note: Frequent tax law changes can modify this deduction. The Tax Reform Act of 1986 made such gifts subject to alternative minimum tax rules. Consult your CPA for details.)

I could tell many horror stories about those I have counseled who thought they could outsmart the IRS. To my knowledge, none succeeded. Most ended up paying the taxes, plus interest and penalties, and lost the investment money as well.

I recall a young real estate salesman named Carl who had been investing in apartment buildings with several other Christians from his church. Carl managed the complexes for which he received a monthly fee. The investors were allocated the tax write-offs for depreciation, taxes, interest, and so on.

As the buildings appreciated in value, Carl would borrow against the equity, sharing equitably with his limited partners. He would then raise the rents to cover the additional loan payments—a great strategy during good times.

But what Carl failed to realize was that he had created a time bomb just waiting for a slump in the economy. Inevitably that slump came, and renters who had lost their jobs moved out.

With the break-even point at 90 percent occupancy, Carl quickly got into financial trouble. Within a few months the apartments were hopelessly delinquent and were being foreclosed by the lenders. After many struggles, with Carl desperately trying to find a way to salvage his investment, the apartments were repossessed. But that wasn't the end of Carl's troubles. The IRS declared that all of the previously claimed depreciation and equity loans would have to be recaptured, meaning that each of the investors would have to claim $50,000 in "phantom" income.

Many of the partners, including Carl, lost everything they owned and still owed thousands in taxes. Carl learned the hard way that you don't really avoid income taxes; you only delay them.

One final note about tax shelters: You should *never* get into an investment solely for the tax benefits involved. Any good investment is eventually supposed to make money for you, and that is the true test that the IRS uses. Did you get into it primarily for economic benefit, or did you get into it primarily to save taxes? If it was primarily to save taxes, the great probability is that you're going to lose money in the investment and that you're going to have to pay back the income tax—with penalties. Remember the caution of Proverbs 28:20: "A faithful man will abound with blessings, but he who makes haste to be rich will not go unpunished."

# 24  KEY #2: AVOID PERSONAL LIABILITY

Most get-rich-quick schemes, as well as most tax shelters, are available only if you accept personal liability for a large debt. God's Word says to avoid *surety*, which means never make yourself personally liable for any indebtedness. For example, let's say that you were going to buy a $10,000 piece of property but had only $2,000 as a down payment. So you put your $2,000 down on the property and then sign a note for the $8,000 that says, "If ever I can't pay this note, the lender has the right to recover his property and sue me for any deficiency." That is surety—taking on a personal liability without a certain way to pay.

On the other hand, let's assume you're buying the same $10,000 piece of property. You put down your $2,000 and sign a note for the additional $8,000. But the condition of the note reads, "If ever I can't pay, the lender has the right to keep what I have already paid in and to recover his property, but I owe nothing additional." In other words, there is no personal liability for any deficiency. In legal terms, that's called an *exculpatory*, meaning that you have limited your liability to the collateral at risk. Thus, you have avoided surety because you always have a definite way to pay: surrender the property. That is the only biblically sound way to borrow.

I would counsel anyone to avoid personal liability at all costs. Then if you buy equipment, property, or investments, the most you can lose is the money you have at risk and not future earnings. Failure to do this can result in the loss of all your family's assets. Many times when an investment goes bad, it does so during the worst times in the economy. That's usually the time when you are least capable of carrying the loss.

I recall an example from the middle 1970s in Atlanta. I was counseling two doctors who were partners together in various real estate ventures. They had the opportunity to buy an apartment complex for about half of its appraised value. All it required was a minimal down payment of $50,000 and signing for the mortgage, which was $1,500,000.

They assured me there was no way the investment could go bad because they could make money with the complex only 50 percent occupied, and it had never been less than 80 percent occupied. The only hitch was that they had to personally endorse the note. In other words, they personally indemnified the lender against any losses. Against my counsel, they both signed the note.

About two years later it was discovered that the complex had urea-formaldehyde insulation in the walls and ceiling. It was condemned, and health officials required that the entire structure be torn down. The insurance paid for a portion of the loss, though it did not cover it all. The doctors were able to sell the land for another portion. But when it was all finished, together they owed nearly half a million dollars.

One of the doctors went bankrupt. The other, who was a Christian, decided he could not go bankrupt and committed to repayment of the loan. As best I know, he's still paying on it. The investment itself was good. The deal was excellent. The only difficulty was that they had to sign personally, which is surety.

Remember the wisdom of Proverbs 22:26: "Do not be among those who give pledges, among those who become guarantors for debts." My counsel is this: don't sign surety, no matter how good the deal sounds.

# 25  KEY #3: EVALUATE RISK AND RETURN

An important factor in investing is called the "risk versus return" ratio. The guideline is this: the higher the rate of return, the higher the degree of risk. You can lower the risk by education and careful analysis, but you cannot eliminate it. The reason any investment pays out a higher rate of return is because it must do so to attract the needed capital.

For instance, an insured CD or a government note may pay 7 percent, while an equivalent corporate bond may pay 10 to 12 percent. Why does a corporate bond pay a higher interest rate than a government note? Because the risk in corporate bonds is higher than in government notes. Before investing in anything riskier than an insured savings account, you need to ask yourself this fundamental question: "Can I really afford to take this risk?"

The answer to that question normally depends on two factors: age and purpose. The older you are, the less risk you can afford to take because it's more difficult to replace the money. But if the purpose of the money is for retirement or education, and both are still years away, you can probably afford to take a higher risk. However, if you need the investment funds to live on right now, then you need the lower risk, regardless of age.

If you are evaluating an investment with a relatively low return, then your risk should be proportionately low as well. Treasury bills, Treasury bonds, certificates of deposit, and the like will yield a relatively low rate of interest, but they also will have a relatively low degree of risk, at least under normal economic circumstances.

If you find an investment that promises a high rate of return but advertises a low degree of risk, watch out; there's no free lunch. As Proverbs 14:18 says, "The naive inherit foolishness, but the sensible are crowned with knowledge."

# 26  KEY #4: KEEP SOME ASSETS DEBT-FREE

As a general rule, I believe you should keep at least 50 percent of all your investments debt-free. This also assumes you are following the guidelines of key #2 and you accept no surety. In other words, the money you have at risk in the investments is all you can lose. You have no contingent liability.

The basic idea is to leverage about half of your investments (without personal liability) in order to hedge against inflation. Your money is actually multiplied through the leverage. With the other half of your investments debt-free, you can never lose everything.

Recently a friend in the real estate development business called to discuss a problem. It seems his business had suffered a large slump due to the economy in his area. As a result of making a commitment to a no-surety plan and keeping at least half of his assets debt-free, he could release the leveraged investments without losing everything.

But he called to ask for advice about selling some of the debt-free investments to help carry some of the other assets. I asked why he would consider selling the debt-free assets to pay on the others. He replied, "I have tens of thousands of dollars in those investments. I really hate to lose them." What he was about to do was exactly what his associates were doing, risking good assets to feed their debts. In their cases, they had little choice because they had endorsed every loan personally and everything was at risk. But in his case there was a choice.

He was literally gambling that the economy in his area would turn around before his assets were exhausted. I gave him my counsel, which was, "Don't risk good assets to feed loans. If they can't pay their way or be sold, let them go."

He followed this advice and is still in business, while most of his associates failed. In fact, he is developing a new business—managing properties for lenders, such as insurance companies and banks that have foreclosed on heavily indebted properties.

# 27  KEY #5: BE PATIENT

A smart investor will keep some cash on hand for emergencies so he or she doesn't have to borrow, no matter what the economy is doing. As a general rule, though, only about 5 to 10 percent of your investments should be in cash or near-cash type investments. These include bonds, certificates of deposit, Treasury bills, and money market funds.

It's important to get your money working for you, but patience will help avoid a great many errors. Remember that most investments look good initially, even the bad ones.

I have never heard of anyone advertising an investment as a really bad deal. Most salespeople think their deal is the best and sincerely believe in their products. It's up to you to sort out the good from the bad.

You must know what your goals and objectives are and select only the investments that help you meet them. Remember this little cliché: greed and speed often work together, so a key to avoiding greed is patience. Most get-rich-quick schemes rely on greed and quick decisions. In fact, there are three basic elements associated with any get-rich-quick scheme:

1. *Attract people who don't know what they're doing.* When you invest in areas you know nothing about, it's difficult to evaluate a good or bad investment. Christians are often very gullible and prone to follow the recommendations of other Christians who don't know what they're doing either.

2. *Encourage people to risk money they cannot afford to lose.* Most people are more cautious with money they have earned than with money they borrow. Borrowed money comes so easy that it's easy to risk.

3. *Attract people who will make investment decisions on the spot.* That's why so many get-rich-quick plans rely on group meetings and a lot of emotional hype. One principle I have found that works is this: if you hear of a deal that sounds so good you don't want to wait and pray about it, pass it up. Good investments are rare and seldom flashy.

I remember a young computer salesman named Chad who called about a deal "too good to pass up." He had called only because his wife pressured him into it. "But we have to see you right away," he said. "I've got to move on this quickly." So I scheduled time to see them the next day.

It seems Chad had a friend who knew a really hotshot computer specialist in Colorado who had developed a program to do stock market trades between the US and European stock exchanges and make profits on the differences.

He was taking in investors and making over 10 percent per month for them. Chad already had cashed in his retirement plan and was about to borrow against the equity in their home. He calculated that he could make enough to start his own business within a couple of years.

His wife, Chris, was panicked to think that he was about to risk $35,000 with someone he didn't even know. Chad said he had talked with several other investors who were making lots of money. He said the developer had paid exactly what he promised every month.

My question was, "Why does he need your money if he's able to make over 100 percent per year? Why doesn't he just borrow the money at 10 percent?"

Chad answered, "He wants Christian investors so that he can get into other ventures in the future." By experience I have found that any investment targeted primarily at Christians is worthy of some suspicion. So I asked Chad if he would mind if I checked this person out.

"No," he replied, but then asked how long it would take because he had to make a decision quickly or the opportunity would be closed. I shared the biblical principles of get-rich-quick with Chad, but it fell on deaf ears. His decision was made. I was just a necessary step to pacify his wife.

In my investigations, I could find nothing on this computer trading genius. If he had learned his trade by handling stocks and bonds, nobody knew about it. I called to get a financial statement and was assured several times that one was "on the way." I could never get even the slightest documentation on what he was doing.

In the meantime, Chad invested $35,000 in this venture and received a check for $3,000 for the first month's profits. The next month he was offered the option of reinvesting the profits, which he did over my objections. He never received the third month's distribution because the state securities commissioner impounded all the "trader's" assets, pending an investigation for securities fraud. It seems he had not been trading stocks at all. He had simply been raising money from gullible people—a *lot* of them.

The system was pretty simple. He paid dividends by raising more money each month. Once someone had received a month or so of distributions he was "allowed" to reinvest his profits, which most did. As long as the circle of investors kept expanding, he had no problems making the payments and pocketing a huge profit. His only overhead was a computer to keep up with the payments.

What blew the whistle was an investor who tried to talk his brother-in-law into investing too. But his brother-in-law was a security investigator who knew a scam when he saw one. Before he folded, this shyster had raised over $20 million and had a list of clients that read like who's who in entertainment, sports, and business.

As Proverb 28:20 says, "A faithful man will abound with blessings, but he who makes haste to be rich will not go unpunished."

The get-rich-quick schemes always look the best initially. If they didn't, nobody would buy them. So be cautious and, above all, be patient. "Rest in the LORD and wait patiently for Him" (Ps. 37:7). Before you do anything, talk about it, pray about it, and then give God time to give you an answer.

# 28  KEY #6: SEEK DIVERSITY

There's an old adage that says, "Don't put all your eggs in one basket." That certainly applies to your investment strategy. Let's assume, for example, that you have a small amount of money to invest, say $1,000, and you want to buy some stock with it. If you put your $1,000 into one company's stock, then all of your money rests on how that one company does. There is an alternative; it's called a mutual fund. In a mutual fund your money is pooled with many others and invested in a variety of different companies. Therefore, you achieve diversification merely by selecting a mutual fund as opposed to just one company.

I would also suggest splitting your money into different areas of the economy. For example, one part might be in real estate, some in gold and silver, a percentage in stocks and bonds, and the remainder in CDs. This helps buffer you from cyclical ups and downs.

For instance, if the price of stock goes up and you have all your money in the stock market, you'll do great. But if you hit a downturn in the stock market and needed to cash out, the result would be a significant loss. However, if you have only a portion of your money in the stock market, another portion in the bond market, some in real estate, some in gold and silver, and so on, the probability is that when one of these areas is down, another will be up. So rather than having to sell the one that's down, you can sell one that's up.

A good adage to remember is one that investor Bernard Baruch used very wisely: "When everybody else is selling, it's time to buy, and when everybody else is buying, it's time to sell." What you should strive to do is buck the trends rather than be forced to go with them.

Let me use another example. Assume you had $10,000 to invest. You might split the money, with $5,000 going into stocks and $5,000 going into bonds. Assume the stocks are inflating because the economy is growing rapidly. Normally the bonds would be devalued as the economy expands. You wouldn't want to sell the bonds. So if you needed cash, you'd sell some stock. But if the economy reversed and interest rates went down rather than up, the stock could drop and the bonds improve in value. Obviously, it's not always as ideal as my example implies, because sometimes both stocks and bonds can go sour at the same time. That's why further diversification is usually necessary.

I've counseled many couples who have adopted this principle. Not long ago, I counseled a couple in which the husband had worked for the same company all of his adult life. His entire life savings and retirement funds were in that company's stock. Though it was a very good company and its stock was sound, everything this couple had to live on for the rest of their lives was at risk in that one company. If the company failed, as any company can, they would have lost their life savings with virtually no chance to replace it. My suggestion to them was to begin to diversify. Sell off some of the stock as they could and put a part of it into mutual funds, a part into land, a part into residential real estate, and so on. By doing so, they would ensure that their savings would not be wiped out if the company's stock dropped drastically.

The principle of diversification is not a onetime decision; you don't diversify and then forget it. You have to continue managing your money. You are required to be a steward of God's property. If you don't have the knowledge, you need to gain it. Spend an hour a day for six months studying any area of investing, and you'll know more than most people who sell it.

To diversify your investments, you need to understand how a multitiered plan works. I'll demonstrate this system when we discuss specific investments, but, briefly, I use five tiers:

- Tier #1 is secure income: CDs, stocks, government bonds, and notes.
- Tier #2 is long-term income: investments that are higher risks but have a higher rate of return, such as mortgages or corporate bonds.
- Tier #3 is growth investments: mutual funds, utility stocks, and gold funds.
- Tier #4 is speculative growth investments: development property, limited partnerships, and new businesses.
- Tier #5 is pure speculation investments: oil and gas, precious metals, and gemstones.

Depending on your age, income, and temperament, you may want to omit one or more of these levels in your planning. For instance, an older person may not want or need to get into tier #5— the purely speculative area. A younger person may not want to get into tier #1—the purely secure income.

Some of the examples we'll look at should help clarify what levels fit best for differing circumstances.

# 29 KEY #7: FOLLOW LONG-RANGE TRENDS

Invest with an eye to long-range economic trends, especially inflation. So many times we get trapped into following short-range trends. When the economy is doing well and inflation and interest rates are down, everything seems to be going great, so everybody wants to jump into the market and make a lot of money.

Some people who get in will make money, but the vast majority who get in are going to panic during a short-term downturn and lose most or all of the money they made, especially if they borrowed to invest. When the market drops, they can't afford to ride it out, so they sell in a down market. So it's always important to think in terms of long-term economics when you evaluate where to put your money. Remember with long-term trends that whatever is going on right now will eventually reverse. Your investments should not stay stagnant, but don't panic when they fluctuate either.

Again, Bernard Baruch said, "There is a strange phenomenon practiced by most investors that most people tend to panic when their assets decline in value, and they will sell simply because they have not taken a long-range view of things."

Perhaps the most significant economic trend that has affected the area of investments over the last ten years has been inflation, and over the next ten it will be either inflation or the threat of depression—or perhaps both. Our primary weapon in fighting a depression is the expansion of credit, which leads a full circle back to inflation again.

So for the years 1990 to 2000, prudent investors who would like their resources to be available in the next decade must hedge both possibilities—inflation and depression.

In a noninflationary economy, you can put your money in a Treasury bill or certificate of deposit and stay even with the economy. But in an inflationary economy, unless you have your money at risk in things that are being inflated with the economy, your buying capacity is eroded.

For example, during the seventies, the most inflation-vulnerable investments were primarily stocks, bonds, savings accounts, Treasury bills, and most other "near-cash" investments. Stocks proved vulnerable primarily because the inflation growth went to the real estate markets. The mideighties saw the stock market recover some of the earlier inflationary growth but only at the price of great volatility.

The most inflation-proof investments over several decades have been real assets: things you can use and touch, such as land, metals, apartment buildings, or houses. During the periods when inflation and interest rates are down, many of the paper investments, such as stocks and bonds, do very well. During this time people tend to forget about inflation. That can be a costly mistake in a debt-run economy. When inflation turns around and interest rates increase to combat it, years of growth can be wiped out in a few months.

# 30  KEY #8: FOCUS ON WHAT YOU OWN

In 1975 I was counseling many people who were wiped out during the economic downturn in the Atlanta area. Many were men who had a significant net worth. And if you looked at them on paper, they looked great financially. Unfortunately, most of their assets were tied up in liabilities and were illiquid. In other words, they didn't have any cash. Their assets were leveraged and required regular payments, and when the payments came due but could not be met, they lost everything.

Almost exactly the same thing happened in the oil industry during the mid-1980s. Men whose net worth was in the millions lost everything they owned, including their homes.

I recall an oilman I met in the late seventies. He was a committed believer and a member of the Christian Oilmen's Association. He had gotten into the oil business just before the oil embargo and had seen the price of oil go from about $6 a barrel to over $30. It seemed that everything he touched turned to gold, and he was thoroughly hooked on the Christian "prosperity message." He actually believed that his giving guaranteed him immunity from economic problems.

As I got to know him, I found that he was worth millions through the oil leases he owned, as well as several drilling operations. But everything was leveraged to the limit. He used every increase in oil prices to borrow more against his reserves so that he could expand further.

When I challenged him on the principle of surety, he became very defensive and ducked behind the normal Christian escape: "God told me to do it." He said that he prayed regularly about every decision and that God confirmed his actions through the increase in his assets. He had also adopted a good-economy mentality. He believed the economy would continue to inflate and carry oil prices with it. What he didn't realize was that much of the inflation was due to the increasing oil prices.

The early eighties saw the price of oil plummet as the oil cartel fell apart. At the same time the new president, Ronald Reagan, waged a war against inflation through high-interest rates to choke off the money supply. Also about this time worldwide conservation began to reduce the demand for oil. This triple blow crippled the oil industry.

The mainline companies such as Shell, Texaco, and Gulf did fine with their preinflation oil leases, but most of the new ventures got wiped out, including this Christian oilman. He could have cashed out in 1970 with perhaps $20 million, yet in 1986 he saw his home and furnishings auctioned off by the court.

You see, your net worth doesn't mean anything. It's how much you actually own unencumbered by liabilities. Have a goal that at least half of your assets will be totally debt-free. If you can't do that right now, make it your number one long-range goal. How can you do it? By saying, "The next time I sell an investment, I'll use that to pay off another investment." As the Lord said, "For which one of you, when he wants to build a tower, does not first sit down and calculate the cost to see if he has enough to complete it?" (Luke 14:28).

# 31   KEY #9: KNOW WHERE TO SELL

Before you buy, always know where you can sell the investment. This key is very important when you're dealing with so-called "exotic" investments such as gemstones, silver, gold, or collectibles. You can do very well buying these items if you know what you're doing. But most people who buy collectibles have no idea of where or how to sell them.

For example, suppose that the precious metals market is doing very well and that you want to sell an antique silver plate. Let's arbitrarily assume that silver is being quoted at $7 an ounce. The first thing you will discover is that your plate is probably worth a lot more than its silver content, based on what you paid for it as an antique. So the price quoted on silver has little meaning. The market for your plate would be to a collector, and normally through an antique broker. Many novice collectors have discovered, to their dismay, that the price they paid for an object was retail (or more) and that the price they're offered is wholesale (or less).

Even if your investment in silver had no collectible value and you tried to resell it for the silver content, you would probably get a shock. First, you would need to have your plate melted down and smelted into nearly pure silver, for which you would pay a fee. Then you would find that no dealer would give you $7 an ounce. Instead they would offer only 75 to 80 percent of that amount. You might make money, but it would require a gain of more than 20 percent to do so.

Let's assume that you bought gold in bullion form. Unless you have an agreement with the sales company that it will buy it back from you, you may have a difficult time even selling your gold. If you do sell it, and gold is being quoted for, say, $400 an ounce, you will discover that a broker won't give you $400 an ounce for it. In fact, he may offer as little as $350 an ounce even though it's certified bullion. Why? Because he needs to make a commission on it too.

Other collectibles, such as figurines, paintings, stamps, and coins are very difficult for a novice to sell profitably. When you invest in these, you need to have a clear understanding of how and where you can sell them. I have counseled many people who said, "Well, the

salesman told me that if I ever wanted to sell, he would buy it back."
Then later they find out that their salesman is no longer around. You'd
better be sure you know an alternate sales source in the event that the
salesperson or company you bought through is gone. Even if they have
been in business for fifty years, they can still fold, especially in a bad
economy. Usually average investors are better off staying with less
exotic investments that have multiple markets available.

# 32  KEY #10: TRAIN FAMILY MEMBERS

Every family member should be trained in the principles of sound
investing.

Statistically in America, a wife is likely going to outlive her
husband. That's an important key to remember when developing an
investment portfolio. I have counseled enough widows, especially
young widows, to know that most of them have no concept of how
to manage any kind of investment program. Many times, because
they don't understand the investments, they will liquidate at the
wrong time and suffer significant losses. So a wife needs to be trained
in good money management and investment strategies. She needs to
know how to buy and sell and where to go for the help she needs.
It is poor stewardship for a wife not to understand the investment
portfolio.

Also, since it is not uncommon for a husband and wife to die
together in an accident, older children should be brought into family
decisions involving your investments. At a minimum, you need to
leave them instructions so they will be able to manage your portfolio

without having to dispose of it upon your death just to pay estate taxes.

# 33  INVESTMENT STRATEGY

We have completed the ten keys to good investing, and now I'd like to discuss a few of the investments available. Understand that what you read should be taken as guidelines to help you get started and not as absolutes. Ultimately any and all investment decisions are yours. As we discuss these investments, we'll look at them in terms of risk and return.

Before proceeding, a few definitions are in order. First, both income and growth are included under the general term *return*. In other words, you may have cash income from a certificate of deposit, and you may have growth income from a rental house—both are considered return on investment. The first is immediate and the second is long term. *Income* means the average current yearly yield. *Growth* refers to the average yearly appreciation of the underlying investment. Therefore, if you get a 5 percent cash return from a rental house after all expenses are paid, and the house is also appreciating 5 percent per year, it has a 10 percent per year return on investment.

The term *risk* refers to the potential loss. In other words, all things being equal, what is the probability that you will get your money back on an investment? To measure risk and return, I have simply assigned a scale from zero to ten that can be applied to each investment. Zero represents the least return or the least risk, and ten represents the highest risk or highest return. Therefore, an invest-ment with an income potential of zero and a risk factor of ten would represent the worst possible investment. An investment with an income potential of ten and a risk of zero would be the best investment. You can't find those, by the way.

The investments will be divided into five basic tiers.

1. *Secure income*—an investment you would select primarily because it generates cash.

2. *Long-term income*—investments selected for their duration of earnings.

3. *Growth investments*—the investment group that is selected primarily for long-term appreciation. Housing would be an example.

4. *Speculative growth*—a mix between growth and speculation.

5. *Pure speculation*—high-risk investments that are selected for their volatility and growth potential.

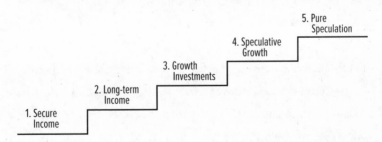

Again, any counsel given in this section is my opinion. It should not be accepted as an absolute. Times and economic conditions are constantly changing, and the kinds of investments that will have a certain degree of return or risk will change with the economy. When interest rates are high and inflation is high, obviously real property, residential housing, apartment complexes, or office buildings generally do well. But when the interest rate and inflation are down, stocks and bonds generally do well. As the economy changes, so do risks and returns.

# 34  TIER #1: SECURE INCOME INVESTMENTS

These are investments that primarily generate income.

**Government Securities.** Included in this group are Treasury bills, GNMA bonds (called Ginnie Mae bonds), and savings bonds. I would give government securities an income of about five, a growth rate of zero, and a risk of one. In other words, you get a return of five, which is an average return with virtually no risk.

**Bank Securities.** Included here are passbook savings accounts, certificates of deposit, and insured money funds. One advantage of bank investments is that you can get into them with smaller amounts of money. Generally, a Treasury bill will require $10,000 to $25,000, but you can purchase a CD for as little as $1,000. The negatives are that they offer no growth because the payout is fixed and income is all taxable.

Be certain that you invest with a bank that is protected by the FDIC, a savings and loan that is protected by the FSLIC, or a credit union that is insured up to $100,000. If worst comes to worst, the government will print the money to pay what they owe. Bank notes have a somewhat higher degree of risk than a government security. I would give them an income rating of about five and a risk of about three or four. If you were going to risk your money long term and you had a choice of a government security or a bank note, I would recommend the government security because it has the same amount of income and less risk.

# 35 TIER #2: LONG-TERM INCOME INVESTMENTS

There are six major types of long-term investments, which I will briefly describe one at a time.

**Municipal Bonds.** These are bonds issued by a particular municipality, such as the cities of Denver, Atlanta, or Chicago. The primary selling point is that most or all the income from municipal bonds is exempt from federal income taxes and is not normally subject to state income tax in the state where they are issued.

The liabilities of municipal bonds are (1) they have low yields; (2) they normally require a large initial investment; and (3) they are illiquid, meaning that if you have to sell them, you will normally do so at a loss. I would grade these as follows: income about five, risk about a seven to eight. With the exception of buying some municipals for diversification, most people are better off with a government bond as opposed to a municipal bond.

**Mortgages.** A mortgage is a contract in which you lend to buy a home or other real property, and you hold the first mortgage rights to it.

I have an attorney friend who specializes in the resale of mortgages. In other words, someone who has financed a first mortgage resells it to get his money out. These are normally discounted by the seller to yield from 3 to 5 percent above the prevailing interest rates at the time. So if current interest rates on CDs are 7 percent, you could earn 10 to 12 percent through a first mortgage. If a borrower fails to pay, you can foreclose on the property. The liabilities of this kind of investment are (1) they are hard to find—it's usually necessary to know a local attorney or a banker who will handle them; (2) the return on your investment is 100 percent taxable as ordinary income; (3) there is no growth on your principal unless interest rates drop, in which case your mortgage might be worth more; and (4) your money will be tied up for a long period of time, possibly fifteen to twenty years.

I would grade first mortgages as an income of eight, no growth, and a risk of about three to four. The risk is low because you have real property backing up your money.

The key here is the value of the property securing the mortgage. I would suggest that any investment in a first mortgage be backed with property valued at two to three times the outstanding loan.

If you are looking for long-term income, in my opinion, a first mortgage is a good way to invest. If you're selling property that you own debt-free, you might consider taking a first mortgage for the amount you were going to invest for income purposes. You can earn a higher rate of interest with less risk than virtually any other investment.

**Corporate Bonds.** A corporate bond is a note issued by a corporation to finance its operation. If the corporation defaults, the assets of the entire corporation can be attached. The liability of this type of investment is that if the corporation files for bankruptcy, your bond is included in the bankruptcy proceedings along with all the other corporate debts.

Some bonds pay a rate of 2 to 3 percent higher than a CD or T-bill. The amount of return depends on the rating of the company issuing the bond. Bonds are rated from a low of C to a high of AAA.

The higher the grade of the bond, normally the lower the rate of return but also the lower the risk.

Many investors prefer bonds that generate current income through their business operations, such as utility bonds with utility companies. In the past, utility company bonds have been very stable and predictable. However, many utilities have suffered massive debts from nuclear power station construction, which has made them greater risks. In general, most utility bonds are still safe investments.

One liability of any corporate bond is that it is dependent on the success of one company. If that company has a problem, your bond can have a problem. Another negative is that the income is 100 percent taxable. A bond has little chance for growth unless your rate of return is in excess of the current interest rate. I would give corporate bonds an income of six to eight and a risk of five to six. The rate of return obviously depends on the prevailing interest rates, and the degree of risk is relative to the grade of the bond.

**Insurance Annuity.** This investment requires a prescribed amount of money to be paid into the annuity, and then the issuing insurance company promises you an income each month upon retirement.

The advantages of investing in annuities are (1) they provide tax-deferred income—the earnings are allowed to accumulate, tax deferred, until you retire; (2) the investment is fairly liquid in that if you have to get some of your money out you can, although there is often a penalty; and (3) relative to other tax sheltered investments, the returns are good.

But be aware that the stated yield of an insurance annuity is not necessarily what you will receive. Sometimes the percentage given is a gross figure, and there are sales and administrative costs to be deducted. It's best to ask for a net figure to do your comparisons. Be sure to get all quotes in writing from the agent offering the annuity. I would give an insurance annuity an income rating of about three to four, primarily because it is a fixed return payable at a future date, and a risk rating of five to six.

**Stock Dividends.** Common stocks usually pay dividends based on the earnings of the company. Stocks have the advantage of being sold for relatively small amounts of money. In other words, it is possible to invest in a stock paying a dividend of 7 to 8 percent and have to risk only $25. Quite often this appeals to the small investor. The dividend or return on investment is totally related to the success of the issuing company. I would look for a company that has paid dividends for many years, particularly during economic hard times.

I personally believe the liabilities of relying on stock dividends for income outweigh the advantages. For one thing, all stock dividends are ultimately dependent on the company's profits. Just because a corporation has paid dividends for decades doesn't necessarily mean it can continue to do so. The automobile industry in the early eighties is a good example. Some of the companies that had paid high rates of return for three to four decades had to cut their returns drastically. Many eventually recovered, but the people who depended on their dividends went through some lean times. So if you're going to invest in stocks for income, you need to assess the degree of risk.

I would rate dividend income at four to five. There can also be growth because the stock can appreciate. I would rate the risk at about six to seven. It's a good place to put some money, but not for those needing income.

**Money Funds.** Money funds are pooled savings accounts. Basically they pool the savings of many people and use their funds to purchase short-term securities. These are not true savings accounts. They are short-term mutual funds that pay interest. The value of the shares you buy are normally $1 per share but can vary depending on the fund's asset value. Most are not insured against losses, but, on the plus side, you can invest as little or as much as you desire into them. Money funds are available through most brokerage firms, savings and loans, or banks. The interest rates vary directly with the current interest rates.

Money funds have a higher degree of risk than the large banks or credit associations. I would rate their income at four to five and the risk factor at seven to eight. In my opinion, money funds are a place to park money temporarily.

# 36 TIER #3: GROWTH INVESTMENTS

This tier is in the middle and thus represents the crossover from the conservative to the speculative. During one cycle of the economy these investments appear to be conservative. Then during the next cycle they appear to be speculative.

A good example of this is farmland. During the highly inflationary seventies, farmland was a hot investment. People speculated in farmland just as they did in commercial real estate. This drove prices up and, unfortunately, tempted farmers to speculate in land.

The eighties saw inflation subside and farm prices level out. Consequently, farmland prices fell also. Today an investment in farmland is considered conservative, and any real growth is viewed as ten or more years out. This can and will change again as the economy changes.

**Farmland.** Developed farmland was consistently one of the best investments in America during the decades of the sixties and seventies. It could well be a great investment again in the future. But if you're investing for growth, you need to realize there is a high degree of risk. The income potential of farmland is basically zero to two. Growth is probably about six to seven over the next ten to fifteen years, and the risk of losing money is probably three to four. I would say as an area of growth, it is a good risk investment, but only if you intend to leave your money there for a long period of time.

**Housing.** Investing in single-family rental houses remains a great option for the average investor. This might not always be the case in the future, but I can see no long-range trends away from rental housing.

In practical fact, housing costs are out of the price range of most average young couples. Since they have to live somewhere, most of them are going to rent, at least temporarily. One advantage of investing in rental housing is that you can do it with a relatively small initial down payment. If you take on the liability of a rental house, be sure not to accept surety for it. If the house won't stand for its own mortgage, pass it by.

Most rental housing generates income and also offers tax shelter through depreciation, interest, taxes, and so on. The Tax Reform Act of 1986 placed limits on what can be deducted for tax purposes against ordinary income, and it's entirely possible that future tax changes will affect real property even more. Still, I believe rental housing will continue to have a good promise of growth, barring an economic catastrophe.

On the other hand, the negatives of rental housing are several: (1) if you don't want to be a landlord, don't buy rental housing; (2) if you aren't able to maintain and manage your own property, many of the tax benefits decline; and (3) it's not always easy to get your money out if you need it. Rental housing really only makes sense if you're willing to put your time and labor into it.

**Duplexes and Triplexes.** The asset of a duplex or triplex is that your income is not limited to one renter. In contrast, if your renter moves out of your single-family home, you have 100 percent vacancy.

With a single-family rental, if all the expenses, such as payments, taxes, and maintenance, can't be met on eleven months of income, it's not a good investment generally. The same principle holds true for a duplex or triplex; the difference is that with a duplex, if one renter moves out, you still have 50 percent occupancy. Therefore, the risk is less.

If you don't have the money to get into a duplex or triplex by yourself, there are two alternatives. You can invest in limited partnerships that are offered by individuals who purchase and manage duplexes and triplexes. Or you can invest with another person. For a detailed discussion on the assets and liabilities of partnerships, I would refer you to my book *Using Your Money Wisely*, published by Moody Publishers.

The liabilities with duplexes or triplexes are that they require a higher investment and more maintenance, and you really do become a landlord.

Remember the three key factors about buying any rental property, whether it is a single-family house, duplex, or triplex. They are location, location, and location. The income potential is five to seven, and the risk is three to four.

# 37  TIER #4: SPECULATIVE GROWTH

Next I'll discuss the four major types of speculative growth investments.

**Mutual Funds.** A mutual fund is an investment in which many small investors pool their money and a group of professional advisers invest it for them, usually in the stock or bond markets. There are specialized mutual funds that invest in automobiles, precious metals, utility companies, government securities, and so forth. You can find a mutual fund for almost any area in which you want to invest.

Mutual funds are valuable for the small investor for several reasons: (1) you can risk a relatively small amount of money—many mutual funds require as little as $25 to invest; (2) your money is spread over a large area in the economy; and (3) the return on good mutual funds has averaged more than twice the prevailing interest rates for any ten-year period.

I would encourage any potential investor in mutual funds to go to independent sources and check out the fund first. There are two sources I use regularly and would highly recommend: *Money* magazine and *Consumer Reports*. Both put out an annual review of mutual funds.

As a Christian, you need to be aware that some mutual funds invest in areas that are questionable and some that are blatantly anti-Christian, including pornography and abortion clinics. You should get a prospectus from the mutual fund that you're considering and find out where your money is going.

Another type of mutual fund invests in the bond market. This is primarily designed for income, obviously. I prefer mutual bond funds over buying individual corporate bonds because the risk is then spread out. The funds invest in many corporations, and the failure of one corporation is not going to affect significantly their (or your) income.

There are differences in the fee structure for mutual funds. Some are called *loaded funds*; others are *no-load funds*. A loaded fund means they require the service cost or commission to be paid up front. A no-load fund means they recover the fees over a number of years. These fees can be quite substantial. If you don't plan to leave your money in a mutual fund for at least five years, you probably shouldn't get into one. Whether it's a loaded or a no-load fund, the fees are going to be about the same over any five-year period.

I personally prefer the no-load fund because it allows my money to be earning dividends without the service fees or commissions coming out of the initial investment. But if you decide to withdraw your money during the first five years, even a no-load fund will charge a penalty to cover their fees. Obviously they have administrative overhead and commissions to recover. The income potential is five to seven, and the risk is four to five.

**Common Stocks.** As discussed earlier, one advantage of common stocks is that you can invest with a relatively small amount of money, and the potential exists for sizable growth. The liabilities of common stocks are obvious. First, you can suffer a loss as easily as you can make a profit. Second, stocks require buying and selling to maximize their potential. Most people think they can put their money into a stock and just let it sit without having to manage it. But that is rarely the case today. If you expect to make money in the stock market, you're going to have to manage it. If you're not willing to do that, it's best to stay with other investments. The income potential is twenty-eight, and the risk is seven to eight.

**Precious Metals.** Precious metals such as gold, silver, or platinum can be purchased whether for long-term growth or pure speculation. Long-term growth means that you buy the metal, put it in a safe-deposit box, and let it appreciate (hopefully) for a period of time. The majority of people who do this do so primarily as a hedge against a potential calamity in the economy. I would counsel most investors to put a small amount of their assets in precious metals. In an economy as unstable as ours, they can be a good balance to assets more vulnerable to inflation. When buying and selling anything, especially precious metals, it always is wise to remember what Baruch said: "Buy when they sell. Sell when they buy." Keep a long-term mentality about precious metals—at least those you invest in as a hedge.

Both gold and silver fluctuate with the economy. Gold usually cycles faster and further than silver, primarily because more people trade in it. In general, the cycles of gold run the opposite of the US dollar. So observing the dollar's trends can give clues to the price of gold. The income potential is five to six, and the risk is eight to nine.

**Limited Partnerships.** A limited partnership is one in which you pool your money with another group of investors to purchase an investment, usually in real properties. The investment is managed by a general partner who has the authority to buy and sell. Through the late seventies and early eighties, apartments and office complexes were commonly purchased through limited partnerships. The investment in a limited partnership is no better than the property and the management. The key is to know the general partner's credibility. Usually the success of any venture is dependent on that person's ability to acquire and manage the properties. For all intents and purposes, the limited partners are "silent" investors who are totally dependent on the general partner.

As a limited partner, your liability is normally limited only to the amount of money you have at risk. That is the only kind of limited partnership I would recommend. Other limited partnerships require subsequent annual payments. For instance, it may be a $30,000 investment requiring $10,000 up front and $10,000 for each of two additional years. I would not recommend these because they carry a contingent liability. In the past, limited partnerships in properties, such as apartment complexes, office complexes, or shopping centers, have been excellent investments since much of the benefit was to shelter other income. However, since 1987 most of these benefits have been eliminated gradually, and the tax write-offs can be used only to shelter passive income. For most investors, the risk is high for the return on these types of investments. The income potential is six to seven, and the risk is eight to nine.

# 38   TIER #5: PURE SPECULATION

These are investments that would normally be a relatively small part of any investment plan. Their primary value is their sizable potential appreciation—in other words, speculation. Most generate little or no income and are highly volatile.

My recommendation is to speculate with only a small ratio of your assets, 5 to 10 percent at the most.

**Gold and Silver.** Under tier #4, we discussed investing in gold and silver for long-term growth. There it was used as a hedge against a financial collapse. But you can also invest in gold and silver for short-term speculation. This would be the case in a highly volatile economy in which major changes were occurring, such as the oil crisis in the midseventies. The run-up in silver prices in the late seventies was another example of speculation in precious metals.

Obviously, such events are difficult to predict and are extremely risky. They are for the investor with a strong heart and cash only. Unless you are a professional investor, this probably is not an area in which you want to risk a lot of money. The income potential is incalculable. The risk is nine to ten.

**Oil and Gas.** In the late seventies and early eighties when crude oil prices cycled up, oil and gas investments were the hottest things going. I saw many people investing money in oil and gas who didn't understand the risks involved. The vast majority lost their investment when the prices fell and marginal wells were unprofitable. There is a high degree of risk, particularly in oil exploration.

Many people invested in oil and gas limited partnerships to develop known gas and oil fields. Not only did they lose their money on these investments, but they also discovered they were liable for environmental damages caused by the wells. It ultimately cost them several thousand dollars to clean up the sites. Most would have given their shares gladly to anyone who would bear the cost of cleanup.

Many of the companies they invested with simply shut down their wells because production costs exceeded income.

This kind of investment is not only very risky but usually very expensive. I would rate the income potential a seven to eight, but I would also rate the risk at nine to ten. If you plan to invest in oil and gas, risk only a small ratio of your assets and don't let anybody talk you into risking larger amounts.

**Commodities Market.** Commodities speculation requires a relatively small dollar investment and can bring very high profits, primarily through the use of leverage. A $1,000 investment in the commodities market can control $10,000 worth of contracts (or more) for future delivery. If that sounds good, then there's an old cliché you need to hear: "A fool and his money are soon parted." Approximately one out of every two hundred people who invest in the commodities market ever gets *any* money back. That doesn't mean there was a profit; it means the initial investment was recovered. Investing in commodities is probably the closest thing to gambling that most people ever try. In fact, it is gambling. You can lose everything you own. The income potential is ten plus, and the risk is ten plus.

**Collectibles.** These are antiques, old automobiles, paintings, figurines, and so on. There are a number of advantages to speculating in collectibles. One is that you can use them while you hold them to sell. For instance, you can rebuild antique cars or classic cars, as my son and I do, and drive them while shopping for buyers.

One of the most important prerequisites to investing in collectibles is knowledge. You need to know value before investing. Second, you need to put some time and labor into locating the best places to buy and sell. Third, you must have the capital to wait for just the right buyer. Often novice investors get discouraged and sell out at a loss.

Unless you have a high degree of knowledge in this area, the risk is inordinately high. With most items, such as antiques, automobiles, figurines, and paintings, you can develop the expertise you need by reading and talking with other people. The rate of return on collectibles can easily be ten plus. But the risk of loss is just as great. The only way you can lower the risk is with your personal expertise: knowing how and where to buy and then how and where to sell.

In our case, we got started by another friend who was buying and selling antique cars. We saved a great deal of both time and money by tapping into his knowledge, although, to tell you the truth, we have lost money on some cars. Usually it has been when we bought what we liked rather than what would sell the best. Don't get personally attached to collectibles or they will become purchases rather than investments.

**Undeveloped Land.** In the late seventies and early eighties, a great way to make money was buying undeveloped land to hold for development in growth areas. The advantage of this kind of investment is that it has utility.

Let's assume you buy some residential lots near where you live to sell to potential homeowners. Even if the market in undeveloped lots is not doing well, it is possible to joint venture with a residential builder. He would build on your lots and pay you as the homes sell. So you do have more than one option.

You can make money speculating in undeveloped land, but the risks are high. I probably would grade the income potential on this ten plus, but the return is also potentially high, about eight to nine.

**Precious Gems.** These include diamonds, opals, rubies, sapphires, and the like. One advantage with gems is that they are available for relatively small amounts of money. You can have them mounted into a ring or a pendant and wear them while you're waiting for them to appreciate. The potential risks are very high. For every person I know who made money in gems, I know a hundred who lost money. First, it's very difficult to tell quality gems from average ones. Second, it's very difficult to dispose of gems at a fair price unless you have your own market. For instance, unless you own a jewelry store or know somebody who does, it's sometimes difficult to dispose of them except at wholesale value or below.

Many people have invested in diamonds, believing they were one of the most dependable areas to invest in, only to find that their diamonds are now worth a fraction of what they paid for them. The diamond market went through great turmoil in the late seventies and has not recovered totally. In addition, the value of gems depends on a wide variety of factors such as size, quality, clarity, cut, and color. It is almost impossible for a novice to know the real value of a gem, even with a certified appraisal.

A case in point was a couple who donated a one-carat flawless diamond to our ministry to help develop some materials. They had paid $14,000 for the stone as an investment in the midseventies and had an appraisal from a leading gemologist done, which substantiated the value.

We had the diamond reappraised for resale and found that the cut was flawed, lowering its value to approximately $6,000. The couple's investment, after earning loss, had netted a *negative* 70 percent, and yet they had followed all the counsel they had been given at the time of purchase. The one thing they lacked was a guaranteed buyback. However, since the sales company folded, that would have been of no value either.

So the rule is, stay with what you know or with someone you thoroughly trust.

## CONCLUSION

We have completed the ten keys to successful investing. Obviously, this is not an exhaustive review, but I trust it will provide you with the pointers to get started in an investment strategy once you have your budget under control and develop a surplus. For a more complete discussion of investments, read my book *Investing for the Future*, published by Victor Books.

Many other excellent materials also are available to you, including good books on investing that you can check out of most public libraries. Just be careful about taking their total counsel because so many are based on the leverage principle. You need to evaluate the risk involved with any investment. I hope that in the time we've spent together, I have at least made that abundantly clear. If not, let me repeat it. There are risks involved with any investment. The higher the promised return, the higher the degree of risk. The only way you can lower the risk is through your own personal expertise. You have to know what you're doing.

# APPENDIX A: BALANCING YOUR CHECKBOOK

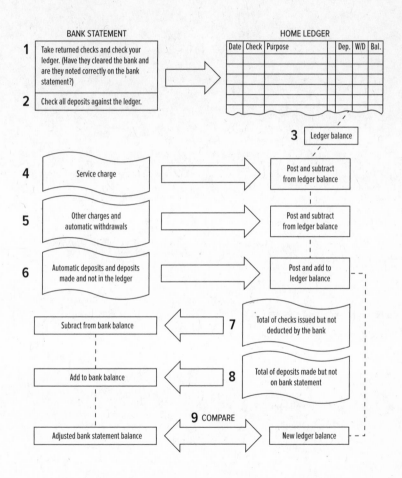

**BANK STATEMENT**

**HOME LEDGER**

| Date | Check | Purpose | | Dep. | W/D | Bal. |
|------|-------|---------|---|------|-----|------|
| | | | | | | |
| | | | | | | |
| | | | | | | |
| | | | | | | |
| | | | | | | |

1 — Take returned checks and check your ledger. (Have they cleared the bank and are they noted correctly on the bank statement?)

2 — Check all deposits against the ledger.

3 — Ledger balance

4 — Service charge → Post and subtract from ledger balance

5 — Other charges and automatic withdrawals → Post and subtract from ledger balance

6 — Automatic deposits and deposits made and not in the ledger → Post and add to ledger balance

7 — Total of checks issued but not deducted by the bank → Subract from bank balance

8 — Total of deposits made but not on bank statement → Add to bank balance

9 COMPARE — Adjusted bank statement balance ↔ New ledger balance

# APPENDIX B: DEVELOPING A BUDGET

## STEP 1

List all the available income. Divide it into income per month.

– Salary _____          – Interest income _____

– Rents _____           – Dividends income _____

– Notes receivable _____   – Income tax or other

refund _____

## STEP 2

List your expenditures in the home on a monthly basis.

| *Variable Expenses* | *Fixed Expenses* |
|---|---|
| – Food | – Tithe |
| – Outstanding debts | – Federal and state income tax (If |
| – Utilities | these are already deducted from |
| – Insurance (life, health, | your pay, ignore this item.) |
| auto, etc.) | – Social Security taxes (Treat the |
| – Entertainment and | same as income taxes.) |
| recreation | – Housing expense (payment/rent) |
| – Clothing allowance | – Residence tax |
| – Medical and dental care | – Residence insurance |
| – Savings | – Other expenditures that are fixed |
| – Miscellaneous | every month: car payments, pay- |
| | ments to support family members, |
| | or any other expense that is pre- |
| | dictable and the same each month. |

If you operate on a nonfixed monthly income, such as sales or commissions, divide the previous year's salary by twelve to get a month-by-month budget income. Do not forget to deduct taxes and other prepayments that are due.

## STEP 3

Compare the categories that you've just noted as income versus expenses. If your total expenses exceed income, you must evaluate every category to decide whether or not you are overspending and, if so, how spending can be reduced. If your income exceeds your total expenses, you must implement a plan that will help you meet your financial goals.

# APPENDIX C: DETERMINING INSURANCE NEEDS

The amount of life insurance a family needs depends on many variables, such as family income, ages of the children, ability of the wife to earn an income, Social Security status, the standard of living you hope to provide, and outstanding debts.

This step-by-step guide (and corresponding worksheet on pages 270–72) will assist you in determining your insurance requirements, which then will have to be weighed against your budget. If the budget dollars are limited, it will be necessary to get as much insurance as possible for the available dollar.

## STEP 1 — PRESENT INCOME PER YEAR
How much income is being provided by the breadwinner of the family? The goal is to provide for the family so they may continue the same standard of living they enjoy under this income.

## STEP 2 — PAYMENTS NO LONGER REQUIRED
Family expenses should drop as a result of the death of the breadwinner. For example, a second car may no longer be required; less income (or different income) will mean less taxes; activities or hobbies would not be an expense; investments or savings may be reduced or stopped.

## STEP 3 — INCOME AVAILABLE
The breadwinner's death may initiate income from some other sources. Social Security income will depend on one's eligibility,

which, in turn, is determined by the time in the system, amount of earnings, and ages of spouse and dependent children. Income may also be available from retirement plans, investments, annuities, or the like.

The income-earning potential of the wife is a definite asset to the family. Ages of the children are a factor here. A minimum insurance program should provide time for obtaining or sharpening job skills if necessary.

## STEP 4 — ADDITIONAL INCOME REQUIRED TO SUPPORT FAMILY

The income presently being earned, less the payments no longer required and less the income available, results in the income needed for the family to continue living on the same level enjoyed through the income of the breadwinner.

## STEP 5 — INSURANCE REQUIRED TO PROVIDE THE NEEDED INCOME

If provision could be made in an ideal manner, the insurance money invested at 10 percent would return the needed amount of income to the family. To find the required amount of insurance, multiply by ten the income required to support the family.

Example: $7,000 additional income is required to
support the family
$7,000 x 10 = $70,000. $70,000 in
insurance invested at 10 percent would
provide the needed funds.

## STEP 6 — LUMP SUM REQUIREMENTS

In addition to the insurance required to produce the regular sustained income, lump sums may be required for specific purposes (for example, college education). Those needs should be determined and added to the total amount of insurance.

Are funds needed to pay off the home mortgage? This should be discussed as a part of the family plan. If mortgage payments are being made under the existing income, then this could be continued under the sustained income provision. Since paying for the home would significantly boost the insurance requirement, this will also raise the amount that must be spent for insurance.

## STEP 7 — ASSETS AVAILABLE

Determine the assets that are available for family provision. Subtract this amount from the desired amount of insurance.

Equity in a home can be counted as an asset only if the survivors plan to sell it.

## STEP 8 — TOTAL INSURANCE NEEDED

The total tells how much insurance is needed. This must be balanced against how much can be spent for insurance. If the insurance dollars are limited, it will be necessary to get as close to the plan as possible with those dollars. Term insurance with its lower initial premiums probably offers the best opportunity for adequate provision with fewest dollars.

The plan should also include instructions as to how the insurance money is to be used.

Note: Insurance needs should be reviewed periodically. Inflation changes or family changes (such as new additions, children becoming employed or leaving home, or income changes) should prompt an insurance review.

### Insurance Needs Worksheet

STEP 1 — PRESENT INCOME PER YEAR                    _____
                                                    Line 1

STEP 2 — PAYMENTS NO LONGER REQUIRED
        Estimated living cost (for deceased) _____
        Life insurance                        _____
        Savings                               _____
        Investments                           _____
        Taxes                                 _____
        _____          _____
        _____          _____

                            Total =           _____
                                              Line 2

INCOME REQUIRED TO SUPPORT FAMILY
        (Line 1 minus Line 2)                 _____
                                              Line 3

STEP 3 — INCOME AVAILABLE
        Social Security                       _____
        Spouse's income                       _____
        Retirement plans                      _____

Investments                          _____

_____              _____

_____              _____

                          Total =        _____
                                          Line 4

## STEP 4 — ADDITIONAL INCOME REQUIRED TO
## SUPPORT FAMILY
(Line 3 minus Line 4)                  _____
                                          Line 5

## STEP 5 — INSURANCE REQUIRED TO PROVIDE THE
## NEEDED INCOME
(Line 5 x 10)                          _____
                                          Line 6

## STEP 6 — LUMP SUM REQUIREMENTS
Debt payments                     _____
Funeral costs                     _____
Estate tax and settlement costs   _____
Education costs                   _____

_____              _____

_____              _____

                          Total =        _____
                                          Line 7

## TOTAL FUNDS REQUIRED
(Line 6 minus Line 7)                  _____
                                          Line 8

## STEP 7 — ASSETS AVAILABLE
Real estate                       _____
Stocks and bonds                  _____

Savings                                    _____

_____                            _____

_____                            _____

                                Total =    _____

                                           Line 9

STEP 8 — TOTAL INSURANCE NEEDED
        (Line 8 minus Line 9)                     _____